중등임용고시 대비

허은성 전공영어
허은성 편저

영어학 ②

Syntax & Grammar

동문사

이 책은 저작권법에 따라 보호받는 저작물이므로 무단전재와 무단복제를 금지하며, 이 책 내용의 전부 또는 일부를 이용하려면 반드시 저작권자와 동문사의 서면동의를 받아야 합니다. 무단전재나 무단복제 행위는 저작권법 제136조(벌칙)에 의거, 5년 이하의 징역 또는 5천만 원 이하의 벌금에 처하거나 이를 병과할 수 있습니다.

혀은성 전공영어 영어학 ②
목차

Intro

교재 구성	004
커리큘럼	005
인사말	006
들어가기에 앞서	007
공부방법	008
예시기출	009

Syntax — 010

Preceding Steps — 011

What is Grammar & Syntax?	012
Syntax as a Science - How Linguists Study Sentence Structure	014
Function-Form Relationships	016
The Structure of English	020
Deep and Surface Structure	024
Tree Diagrams	026
C-command	029

Predicates, Arguments, and Thematic Roles — 033

Predicates and Arguments	034
Thematic Roles	038
Grammatical Functions and Thematic Roles	042
Further Thematic Relations	044
Subcategorization	046
Selectional Restrictions	049

X-Bar Theory — 051

Heads, Complements, and Specifiers (X-Bar Syntax)	052
Adjuncts in X-Bar Theory	055
Cross-Categorial Generalizations in X-Bar Syntax	060
Complements vs. Adjuncts: Extraposition (Postposing)	061
Complements vs. Adjuncts: Preposing	062
The Differences Between Complements and Adjuncts	063

Clauses & Movement — 066

The I-node(Inflectional Node)	067
Affix Movement vs. V Movement	071
I Movement(I-to-C Movement)	076
Trace	079
Wh-Movement	082
NP-Movement in Passive	086
NP-Movement: Subject-to-Subject Raising	090

Syntax

Constituency Tests	**093**
Constituency	094
The Movement Test	095
VP-Topicalization (VP-Preposing): Moving Verb Phrases to the Left	096
Heavy-NP-Shift: Moving Heavy Noun Phrases to the Right	098
Extraposition of Subject Clauses	099
Extrapositionfrom NP(ENP)	100
Substitution(Replacement)	103
The Coordination Test	108
Complementizers	113
The Cleft and Pseudocleft Test	115
The Insertion Test	117
Stand-alone Test (The Constituent Response Test or The Sentence Fragment Test)	119

Verb Complements	**124**
Intro	125
The Believe-Type Construction	127
The Persuade-Type Construction	131
The Want-Type Construction	134
Summary: Verb+NP+to-infinitive construcrion	137

Raising and Control	**138**
Raising and Control Predicates	139
Differences Between Raising and Control Verbs	141
Tough Movement & Subject Raising	145

Control Theory	**143**
Introduction	149
Obligatory vs. Nonobligatory Control	150

Binding Theory	**155**
The Basic Concepts of Binding Theory	156
Coindex and Antecedent	158
Binding	159
Locality Conditions on the Binding of Anaphors	161
The Distribution of Pronouns	163
The Distribution of R-Expressions	164

Case Theory	**165**
Case	166
Complements-Accusative case Assigned by V and P in case Theory	167
Subjects- Nominative and Accusative Case	168
Exceptional Case-marking(ECM)	169
Adjectives and Nouns: of-Insertion	170
Adjacency	171
Passivization	172
The Double Object Construction	175
Movement and Chains	176
Summary: Case Theory in English	177

Grammar 178

Nonreferential There	179
Pronoun	182
Focus	184
Verb Complementation	186
Determiners	191
Stative and Dynamic Senses of Verbs	197
Model Auxiliaries	200
Negation	203
Passive	210
Relative Clauses	216
Coordination	220
Multiword Verbs	227
Adjectives	237
Adverbials	246
Aspect	250

문제 및 정답 256

교재
구성

→ 그날 공부 할 영어학 분야의 제목을
한 눈에 볼 수 있게 구성하였습니다.

→ 영어로 개념 설명을 하여
실전 문제에 대비하게 하였습니다.

What is Grammar & Syntax?

1. What is Grammar & Syntax?
- Grammar refers to the overall system of rules governing a language.
- Syntax is a subfield of grammar that specifically deals with sentence structure.
- The primary focus of syntax is to determine the rules that dictate how

- Existential "there"
There were six policemen on the bus.
There does not refer to a location;
it simply introduces existence.

↓ 다양한 영어학 예시를 사용하여
이해에 도움을 드리고자 하였습니다.

1. Read the passage and follow the directions.

Sentence adverbs such as perhaps, probably, frankly, and definitely modify entire sentences rather than individual verbs or phrases. These adverbs provide syntactic evidence that modal verbs (e.g., will, can, must) are generated under the I-node (Inflectional node), since sentence adverbs can occur between the subject and the main verb, including in positions before or after the modal.

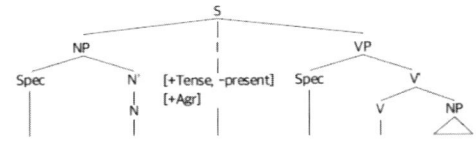

Consider the following sentences using the sentence adverb definitely:

a. Definitely, my sister can solve the problem.
b. My sister definitely can solve the problem.
c. My sister can solve definitely the problem.
d. My sister can solve the problem definitely.

Identify which sentence among (a)–(d) is ungrammatical. Then, provide evidence for your answer based on the explanation of sentence adverbs in the passage.

← 배운 개념을 적용 할 수 있는
문제와 정답을 제공해드립니다.
(강의자료실과 다음카페 업로드)

허은성 전공영어 커리큘럼

	1월	2월	3월	4월	5월	6월	7월	8월	9월	10월	11월
일반영어	Level 1 문제		Level 2 문제		Level 3 기출		Level 4 통합 모의고사		Level 5 통합 모의고사		
문학	Level 1, 2 개념+문제				Level 3 기출						
영어교육론	Level 1, 2 개념+문제				Level 3 기출						
영어학	Level 1~2 개념+문제 (Phonetics, Phonology, Morphology, Semantics, Pragmatics)		Level 1~2 개념+문제 (Syntax, Grammar)		Level 3 기출						
월간 허은성	1월	2월	3월	4월	5월	6월	7월	8월	9월	10월	
특강		다시 배우는 영문법									
			AEP (원서 특강)								
					Transformational Grammar (원서 특강)						
			Teacher's Grammar of English								
				교육전문가 교육 이슈 및 관련 주제 특강							
	위 특강 이외의 특강은 학생들의 의견을 수렴하여 추후 특강 진행 예정										

인사말

미래의 영어 선생님들께,

처음으로 임용 시험 준비를 결심한 여러분께 깊은 존경과 응원의 마음을 전합니다. 새로운 도전을 시작하는 일이 설레기도 하지만, 한편으로는 두렵고 막막하게 느껴질 수 있다는 것을 저도 잘 알고 있습니다. 하지만 여러분이 내딛는 이 첫 걸음은 이미 큰 용기를 보여주는 것입니다.

처음에는 어디서부터 시작해야 할지 막연하게 느껴질 수 있습니다. 하지만 중요한 것은 모든 것을 한꺼번에 잘하려고 하기보다, 차근차근 한 걸음씩 나아가는 것입니다. 기초를 다지고, 목표를 설정하며, 작은 성취를 이루어나가는 과정에서 자신감이 쌓일 것입니다.

임용 시험 준비는 단순히 지식을 쌓는 과정을 넘어, 여러분 자신을 성장시키고 선생님으로서의 자질을 다듬어가는 여정입니다. 이 길의 끝에는 여러분을 기다리는 학생들과 꿈꾸던 교실이 있습니다. 그 생각이 여러분의 발걸음을 더 단단하게 만들어 줄 것입니다.

혹시라도 길을 잃은 듯 느껴질 때, 혹은 지칠 때, 혼자가 아니라는 것을 기억하세요. 여러분 곁에는 함께 걷는 동료들과 제가 있다는 것을 잊지 마세요. 여러분의 시작을 응원하고, 끝까지 함께할 준비가 되어 있습니다.

시작이 반이라는 말처럼, 이미 여러분은 중요한 반을 이뤄냈습니다. 그 용기를 끝까지 잃지 않고, 매 순간 최선을 다한다면, 여러분의 노력은 분명 꿈에 닿을 것입니다.

여러분의 출발을 진심으로 응원하며,

Believe in yourself and all that you are.

여러분을 응원하는 은성쌤이

들어가기에 앞서

영어학 교재의 첫 장을 펼친 여러분을 진심으로 환영합니다. 영어학은 흔히 가장 어렵다고 여겨지는 과목 중 하나로, 처음에는 낯설고 막막하게 느껴질 수 있습니다. 하지만 이 과목을 통해 언어의 구조, 소리, 의미, 그리고 사용에 대해 깊이 이해하게 된다면, 영어학의 기반을 더욱 탄탄히 다질 수 있는 귀중한 기회를 얻게 될 것입니다.

공부를 시작하며 분명 어려움이 있을 수 있지만, 그 어려움은 결코 극복할 수 없는 것이 아닙니다. 여러분의 꾸준한 노력과 의지, 그리고 이 교재를 활용한 체계적인 학습을 통해 우리는 함께 이 과정을 헤쳐 나갈 수 있습니다.

여러분은 할 수 있습니다. 때로는 두렵고 스스로를 의심하는 순간이 찾아올 수도 있지만, 그 순간조차 성장의 기회로 삼으세요. 도전은 여러분을 더 강하고, 더 지혜롭고, 더 준비된 교사로 만들어줄 것입니다.

성공이란 어려움이 없는 상태가 아니라, 어려움 속에서도 끝까지 나아가는 힘에서 비롯됩니다. 이 교재와 함께, 여러분의 노력과 끈기로 목표를 향해 한 걸음씩 나아가기를 바랍니다. 여러분의 꿈을 향한 여정을 진심으로 응원합니다.

함께 한 걸음씩 나아갑시다!

진심을 담아,
허은성

2025. 1. 2.
여러분을 응원하는 은성쌤이

공부방법

영어학은 언어의 구조와 기능을 깊이 탐구하는 과목으로, 처음에는 복잡하고 낯설게 느껴질 수 있습니다. 하지만 올바른 접근법과 꾸준한 학습을 통해 충분히 극복할 수 있습니다. 다음은 영어학을 효과적으로 공부하기 위한 방법입니다.

1. 기본 개념부터 탄탄히 다지기

영어학의 주요 분야(음성학/음운론, 형태론, 통사론, 의미론, 화용론 등)를 이해하려면 먼저 기초 개념에 집중하세요. 용어와 개념을 정확히 이해하고 이를 설명할 수 있어야 합니다.

2. 도식화와 체계적인 정리

영어학은 복잡한 구조를 다루므로, 학습 내용을 도식화하고 정리하는 것이 중요합니다. 트리 다이어그램, 음성 기호표, 의미망 등을 활용하면 시각적으로 내용을 이해하기 쉬워집니다.

3. 이론을 실전 문제에 적용하기

이론 학습 후에는 문제를 풀며 이해도를 점검하세요. 영어학은 단순 암기 과목이 아니라, 분석하고 적용하는 능력이 요구됩니다. 기출문제를 통해 자주 출제되는 유형을 파악하고, 스터디를 통해 직접 문제를 만들어보는 것도 좋은 방법입니다.

4. 학습 루틴 만들기

영어학은 하루아침에 완성되지 않으므로, 매일 정해진 시간에 꾸준히 학습하는 것이 중요합니다. 특히, 복습을 통해 학습 내용을 장기 기억에 저장하세요.

5. 스터디와 상호 학습

혼자 공부하는 것도 좋지만, 스터디 그룹을 통해 서로 토론하며 배운 내용을 점검하고, 이해하지 못한 부분을 보완할 수 있습니다.

7. Read the passage and follow the direction

<A>

In general, the matrix subject is semantically associated with the matrix verb, which is called an *ordinary* subject. In (1a), *Chris* experienced the feeling of wanting to convince Max. In some cases, the matrix subject does not have a direct semantic relationship with the matrix verb, but semantically it belongs solely in the embedded clause. This is called a *raised* subject. The meaning of (1b) is very close to that of *Chris seemingly convinced Max.*

(1) a. Chris wanted to convince Max.
    b. Chris seemed to convince Max.

There are diagnostic tests to distinguish one from the other, which include using meaningless dummy pronouns and voice transparency. First, a dummy pronoun, such as *there* or *it*, cannot appear in the ordinary subject position, as shown in (2a), which suggests that the subject of *want* is an ordinary subject. In contrast, the pronoun can appear in the raised subject position, so the appearance of *there* in (2b) suggests that the subject of *seem* is a raised subject.

(2) a. *There wants to be plenty of time.
    b. There seems to be plenty of time.

The second diagnostic test involves voice transparency between active and passive forms, and only the sentence with a raised subject can denote the same meaning with its passive counterpart. Consider the sentences (3a) and (3b), which are the passive counterparts of (1a) and (1b), respectively.

(3) a. Max wanted to be convinced by Chris.
    b. Max seemed to be convinced by Chris.

Note that (3a) does not share the same truth condition with (1a) as the subject of want refers to Max in (3a) but Chris in (1a). In contrast, (3b) is logically equivalent to (1b). Thus, the test results for voice transparency demonstrate that the subject of want is an ordinary subject and that of seem is a raised subject. Now, consider the sentences (4a) and (4b).

(4) a. The fire fighter attempted to save the man.
    b. The fire fighter happened to save the man.

The two diagnostic tests can reveal that (4a) contains a(n) ① subject and (4b) contains a(n) ② subject.

Note: '*' indicates the ungrammaticality of the sentence.

Fill in the blanks ① and ② each with the ONE most appropriate word from the passage, in the correct order. Then, first, for the raised subject in (4), explain your answer by providing a sentence with a meaningless dummy, using the structural frame, 'to rain'. Second, for the ordinary subject in (4), explain your answer by providing a sentence, using voice transparency.

Syntax

Preceding steps

What is Grammar & Syntax?

1. What is Grammar & Syntax?

- Grammar refers to the overall system of rules governing a language.
- Syntax is a subfield of grammar that specifically deals with sentence structure.
- The primary focus of syntax is to determine the rules that dictate how words are arranged to form grammatical sentences.

2. Word Order in Syntax

A key aspect of syntax is word order. In English, words must follow a strict order to form grammatical sentences. The passage provides three examples:

The President ate a doughnut. (Correct)
*The President a doughnut ate. (Incorrect word order)
*Doughnut President the ate a. (Incorrect word order)

English follows a Subject-Verb-Object (SVO) order, and deviations from this pattern result in ungrammatical sentences.

3. Constituency in Syntax

The passage above(2. word order in syntax) introduces the concept of constituents, which are groups of words that function as a single unit within a sentence. Constituents are important because they:

- Group words together logically (e.g., "the President" behaves as a unit).
- Can be substituted by pronouns (e.g., "The President" → "He").
- Help us analyze sentence structure in a meaningful way rather than simply listing individual words.

Example: Identifying Constituents

Consider the sentence:
- The President blushed.

One way to analyze it is by separating individual words:
- The – President – blushed

However, this does not reveal how words relate to each other.
A better analysis groups words into meaningful units:
- [The President] – [blushed]

[The President] is a noun phrase (NP) referring to an individual.
[blushed] is a verb phrase (VP) describing an action.

This is confirmed by substitution:
- [He] – [blushed]

Since "He" replaces "The President", we confirm that "The President" is a single unit (a constituent).

Key Takeaways

- Syntax studies sentence structure, focusing on word order and hierarchical relationships between words.
- Word order is essential in English, as it follows a strict SVO pattern.
- Constituents are meaningful units within sentences and can be tested through substitution.
- Brackets ([ ]) indicate constituent structure, showing how words form logical units in a sentence.

Syntax as a Science

How Linguists Study Sentence Structure

1. How Syntax Follows the Scientific Method

Syntax, like other sciences, follows a systematic approach to studying language. Linguists (syntacticians) apply the scientific method by:

- Observing language data (e.g., sentence structures in a language).
- Identifying patterns (e.g., in English, subjects typically come before verbs in statements).
- Developing a hypothesis based on these patterns.
- Testing the hypothesis with more language data.
- Revising the hypothesis if new evidence contradicts it.

This method helps linguists refine their understanding of how sentences are structured.

2. Why Hypotheses in Syntax Must Be Testable

For a hypothesis to be useful in syntax (or any science), it must:

- Make predictions about what sentences should be grammatical or ungrammatical.
- Be falsifiable, meaning it can be tested and proven wrong if necessary.

For example:
- If a hypothesis predicts that a sentence should be correct, but native speakers reject it, the hypothesis must be revised.
- If a hypothesis predicts that a sentence should be incorrect, but speakers accept it, it also needs adjustment.

3. Hypotheses in Syntax: Rules and Grammar

- In syntax, hypotheses take the form of rules.
- The set of all syntactic rules in a language is called grammar.

Many people misunderstand grammar because there are two different ways to define it:

① **Prescriptive Grammar** - Rules that tell people how they should speak. These are enforced by teachers, editors, and language authorities.

Examples:
"Never end a sentence with a preposition."
"Use whom, not who, in certain contexts."
"Don't split infinitives."

These rules prescribe what is considered proper according to formal standards.

② **Descriptive Grammar** - Rules that describe how people actually speak. Linguists observe real-world language use without judging correctness.

Example: Many English speakers naturally say, "Who are you talking to?" even though prescriptive grammar discourages ending sentences with prepositions.

Key Takeaways

- Syntax is studied scientifically, using observation, hypothesis, and testing.
- Good syntactic hypotheses must be falsifiable—they should predict patterns that can be tested.
- Syntactic rules function as hypotheses, and grammar is the collection of all these rules.
- Prescriptive grammar tells people how they should speak, while descriptive grammar explains how they actually speak.

Function-Form Relationships

1. Understanding Function and Form

- Function in syntax refers to roles like Subject, Direct Object, Adjunct, etc.
- Form refers to word classes (noun, adjective, verb, etc.), phrases (NP, VP, PP, etc.), clauses (matrix clause, subordinate clause), and sentences.

To understand this distinction, consider the analogy of everyday objects and their functions:

- A computer can be used for word processing, calculations, or sending emails.
- The function of transportation can be fulfilled by a car, train, bus, bicycle, etc.

Similarly, in language, there is no one-to-one relationship between form and function:

- The same form (e.g., a noun phrase) can fulfill different functions (e.g., Subject or Direct Object).
- The same function (e.g., Subject) can be expressed by different forms (e.g., NP, PP, or a clause).

2. Realizations of the Subject

A Subject can be realized by different forms:

① Noun Phrases (NPs) as Subjects

- [NP The hedgehog] ate the carrot.
- [NP A rat] bit my toe.
- [NP This shoe] hurts me.
- [NP Teachers] never lie.

② Prepositional Phrases (PPs) as Subjects

Subjects can also be realized as Prepositional Phrases (PPs), though with some restrictions:

- [PP Under the stairs] was a safe area to be during the war.
- [PP Outside the fridge] is a bad place to keep milk.

PPs as Subjects are often locative (place-related).

- [PP After Saturday] would be a good time to go away for a few days.
- [PP Between eleven and midnight] suits him.

PPs as Subjects are often time-related.

The main verb in such sentences is frequently (though not always) the verb be.

③ Finite Clauses as Subjects
- [That he will go to New York soon] is obvious.
- [That this policy is ludicrous] doesn't need to be demonstrated.
- [What the terrorists said] puzzled the police.

④ Non-finite Clauses(infinitive clauses) as Subjects
- [For us to understand the issues] requires a major mental effort.
- [To be a good teacher] is more difficult than people think.

3. Realizations of the Direct Object

A Direct Object can also be realized by different forms:

① Noun Phrases (NPs) as Direct Objects
- Monica admires [NP the President].
- Ralph enjoys [NP her company].
- Nina described [NP the event].

② Prepositional Phrases (PPs) as Direct Objects
Although less common, some PPs can function as Direct Objects:
- Speaker A: Where will the new discotheque be built?
- Speaker B: I don't know, but the council rejected [PP behind the church].

- Speaker A: Are you going on holiday before or after Easter?
- Speaker B: I prefer [PP before Easter].
  Like PP-Subjects, PP-Direct Objects tend to indicate location or time.

Function-Form Relationships

③ **Finite Clauses as Direct Objects**
- The government believes [that the voters are stupid].
- Maggie doubts [that her boyfriend will ever change].
- He knows [what she means].
- They finally decided [where they will send their child to school].

4. The Lack of a One-to-One Relationship Between Function and Form

The central idea in this section is that form and function do not have a fixed one-to-one relationship.

Example: The Changing Role of "The Cat"
- The cat devoured the rat.
  The cat functions as the Subject.

- The rat devoured the cat.
  The cat now functions as the Direct Object.

Thus, the same NP ("the cat") can serve different syntactic functions depending on word order.

5. Levels of Sentence Analysis

A sentence can be analyzed at different levels:

Example: David smashed the window.

At three levels of description, this can be represented as follows:

Level	Representation
Syntax (structure)	David smashed the window.
Function (roles)	Subject - Predicate - Direct Object
Form (categories)	[S [NP N] [VP V [NP Det N]]]
Semantics (meaning)	Agent - Predicate - Patient

- Syntax shows how words combine.
- Function shows the grammatical role of each part.
- Form shows the structural components (NP, VP, etc.).
- Semantics shows who is doing what
  (e.g., Agent = "David", Patient = "window").

> **Key Takeaways**
>
> - Function refers to grammatical roles (e.g., Subject, Direct Object).
> - Form refers to word categories (e.g., NP, PP, clause).
> - There is no strict one-to-one correspondence between function and form:
>   - The same form (e.g., NP) can serve different functions (e.g., Subject, Direct Object).
>   - The same function (e.g., Subject) can be realized by different forms (e.g., NP, PP, clause).
> - A sentence can be analyzed at multiple levels: syntax, function, form, and semantics.

The Structure of English

1. The Rank Scale

Every sentence can be analyzed at four different structural levels, known as the rank scale:

- Word Level - Individual words.
- Phrase Level - Groups of words forming meaningful units (e.g., noun phrases, verb phrases).
- Clause Level - Groups of phrases forming independent or dependent clauses.
- Sentence Level - A complete sentence, possibly containing multiple clauses.

Linguists use labelled bracket notation to represent these levels.

Example Sentence: Tim thought that Kate believed the story.
Its rank scale representation is as follows:

① Word Level
Each word is assigned a basic category:
[N Tim] [V thought] [Comp that] [N Kate] [V believed] [Det the] [N story]

② Phrase Level
Words are grouped into phrases:
[NP [N Tim]] [VP [V thought] [Comp that] [NP [N Kate]] [VP [V believed] [NP [Det the] [N story]]]]

③ Clause Level
Phrases are combined into clauses:
[MC [NP [N Tim]] [VP [V thought] [SubC [Comp that] [NP [N Kate]] [VP [V believed] [NP [Det the] [N story]]]]]]

④ Sentence Level
The full sentence is represented as a single unit:
[S [MC [NP [N Tim]] [VP [V thought] [SubC [Comp that] [NP [N Kate]] [VP [V believed] [NP [Det the] [N story]]]]]]]

Each level includes the lower levels within it, making the structure increasingly complex.

2. Tree Diagrams

Because labelled bracket notation becomes difficult to read at higher levels, linguists use tree diagrams (also called phrase markers).

For the sentence: Tim thought that Kate believed the story.

A tree diagram visually represents the hierarchical structure, making it easier to see how words group into phrases and how phrases form clauses.

Basic Tree Diagram Structure:

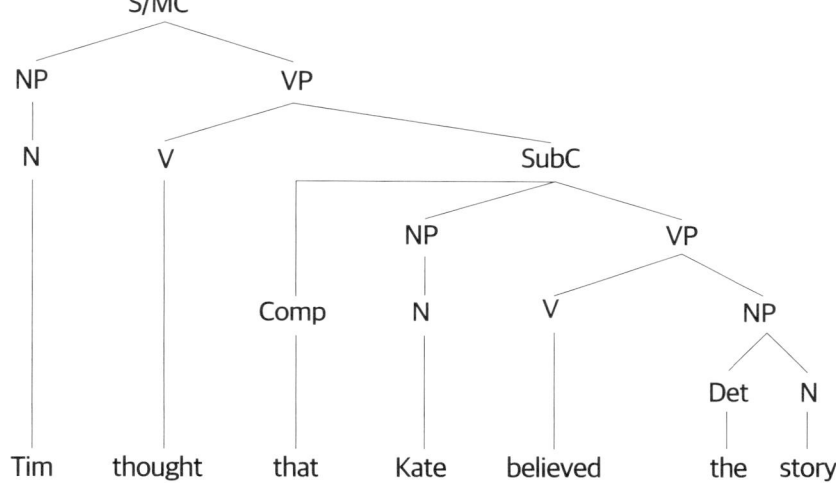

- The sentence (S) consists of a main clause (MC).
- The main clause contains an NP (Tim) and VP (thought that Kate believed the story).
- The VP contains a subordinate clause (SubC) introduced by that.
- The subordinate clause contains another NP (Kate) and VP (believed the story).
- The Direct Object of "believed" is the story, an NP.

This hierarchical representation clarifies sentence structure.

The Structure of English

3. Phrase Structure Rules (PS Rules)

Phrase structure rules describe how sentences are built from smaller units. These rules:

- Specify how words form phrases and how phrases form sentences.
- Are hierarchical and recursive, meaning a phrase can contain another phrase of the same type.

Basic Phrase Structure Rules	
Rule	Description
S → NP VP	A sentence consists of a Noun Phrase (NP) and a Verb Phrase (VP).
VP → V NP / VP → V PP	A Verb Phrase contains a Verb (V) followed by a Noun Phrase (NP) or Prepositional Phrase (PP).
NP → Det N / NP → NP PP	A Noun Phrase contains a Determiner (Det) and a Noun (N) or can be expanded with a PP.
PP → P NP	A Prepositional Phrase consists of a Preposition (P) followed by a Noun Phrase (NP).
AP → Adv A	An Adjective Phrase consists of an Adverb (Adv) modifying an Adjective (A).
ADVP → Adv	An Adverbial Phrase consists of an Adverb (Adv) alone.

Example: Sentence Generation Using PS Rules

Consider the sentence:

The teacher read a book.

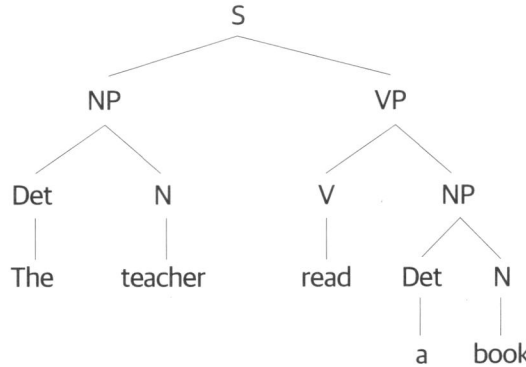

Key Takeaways

- The Rank Scale organizes sentence analysis into four levels: word, phrase, clause, and sentence.
- Labelled bracket notation shows hierarchical structure but can be complex.
- Tree diagrams visually clarify sentence structure.
- Phrase Structure Rules (PS rules) define how words combine into phrases and sentences.
- PS rules are hierarchical and recursive, allowing complex sentence formation.

Deep and Surface Structure

1. Introduction to Deep and Surface Structure

Noam Chomsky originally proposed the Deep Structure and Surface Structure model to explain how sentences are formed and transformed in human language.

- Deep Structure: The underlying, base order of a sentence before transformations.
- Surface Structure: The final, derived form of a sentence after transformational rules apply.

Phrase structure rules determine basic sentence structure, but they do not explain how elements can be rearranged. The Deep and Surface Structure theory accounts for these transformations.

2. The Role of Transformational Rules

When acquiring a language, speakers do not memorize every possible sentence. Instead, they learn rules that generate and modify sentences.
This process follows a general structure:

Deep Structure → Application of Transformational Rules → Surface Structure

3. Movement in Syntax

Movement is a transformational operation that allows phrases to be rearranged under certain syntactic conditions.

Example: Particle Movement
① Deep Structure:
John picked up the book.
② Surface Structure (after movement):
John picked the book up.

- The particle ("up") moves after the object ("the book").
- Both versions are grammatical but involve different word orders.

4. NP Raising (Tough Movement)

NP Raising (or Tough Movement) shifts a noun phrase (NP) to a different position in the sentence.

Example: NP Raising in Tough Constructions
① Deep Structure:
____ is easy to please Julio.
② Surface Structure (after movement):
Julio is easy to please.

- The NP ("Julio") moves from its original position to the subject position.
- This transformation is commonly found in "tough" constructions
  (e.g., "easy to please," "hard to convince").

Key Takeaways

- Deep Structure represents the original, base order of a sentence.
- Surface Structure is the final, transformed version after applying transformational rules.
- Transformational rules allow word order variations, such as movement and NP raising.
- The Deep and Surface Structure theory explains how speakers generate infinite sentences without memorizing them individually.

Tree Diagrams

1. Understanding Tree Diagrams

Tree diagrams are visual representations of sentence structure that show the hierarchical relationships between words and phrases. To describe these relationships precisely, we use specific terminology.

2. Nodes and Dominance

Basic Structure

Consider the abstract tree diagram

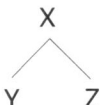

- X, Y, and Z are called nodes.
- X dominates Y and Z, meaning we can trace a line from X to both Y and Z.
- Y precedes Z, meaning Y appears to the left of Z in the tree structure.

Now, consider a more complex tree

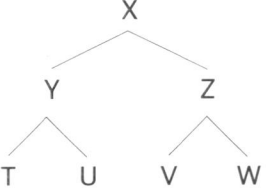

- X dominates all the nodes below it: Y, Z, T, U, V, and W.
- X immediately dominates only Y and Z.
- Y dominates T and U, while Z dominates V and W.

3. Immediate Dominance and Family Terminology

To distinguish different dominance levels, we use immediate dominance.

- X dominates Y, Z, T, U, V, and W, but immediately dominates only Y and Z.
- Y immediately dominates T and U.
- Z immediately dominates V and W.

Using family terminology:
- X is the mother of Y and Z.
- Y and Z are daughters of X.
- Y and Z are sisters.
- T and U are immediate constituents of Y.
- V and W are immediate constituents of Z.

4. Constituents and Immediate Constituents

A constituent is a group of words that form a syntactic unit.

Formal Definition:
Y is a constituent of X if and only if X dominates Y.

- In the tree above, all of Y, Z, T, U, V, and W are constituents of X.
- T and U together form the constituent Y, and V and W together form theconstituent Z.

Immediate Constituents:
Y is an immediate constituent of X if and only if X immediately dominates Y.

- Y and Z are immediate constituents of X.
- T and U are immediate constituents of Y.
- V and W are immediate constituents of Z.

Tree Diagrams

5. Non-Constituent Structures

Consider the following structure:

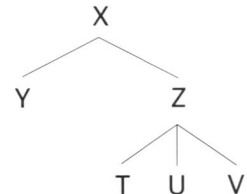

- T, U, and V together form the constituent Z.
- However, T and U alone do not form a constituent.

Why?

A set of nodes A forms a constituent B if and only if B dominates all and only the nodes of A.

- In this case, Z dominates T, U, and V—so T and U alone do not form a constituent.

Key Takeaways

- Tree diagrams show hierarchical sentence structures.
- Nodes represent words or phrases in a sentence.
- Dominance indicates which nodes are higher in the hierarchy.
- Immediate dominance distinguishes direct parent-child relationships.
- Constituents are units in a sentence that function together syntactically and semantically.
- Immediate constituents are directly dominated by a higher node.
- Not all word groupings are constituents—a set of words forms a constituent only if a single node dominates all and only those words.

C-command

1. Understanding C-command

C-command (constituent-command) is a structural relationship in syntactic trees that helps define grammatical dependencies between nodes. It is widely used in syntax to explain phenomena such as binding, movement, and scope interpretation.

Formal Definition of C-command
Node X c-commands node Y if and only if:
- The first branching node that dominates X also dominates Y.
- X does not dominate Y, nor does Y dominate X.

A branching node is a node that splits into two or more constituents.

2. Example of C-command in a Tree Structure

Consider the following syntactic tree:

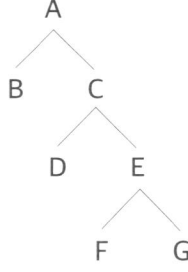

Step-by-step C-command Analysis
- Find the first branching node above a node.
- Determine which nodes are also dominated by that branching node.
- List the nodes that the target node c-commands.

Using this process, we analyze which nodes each node c-commands:
Determining C-command Relations

C-command

We analyze each node:

① A (Root Node)
A c-commands nothing because it is the highest node in the tree.

② B
The first branching node above B is A.
A also dominates C, D, E, F, and G.
Thus, B c-commands C, D, E, F, and G.

③ C
The first branching node above C is A.
A also dominates B, so C c-commands B.

④ D
The first branching node above D is C.
C also dominates E, F, and G.
Thus, D c-commands E, F, and G.

⑤ E
The first branching node above E is C.
C also dominates D, so E c-commands D.

⑥ F
The first branching node above F is E.
E also dominates G, so F c-commands G.

⑦ G
The first branching node above G is E.
E also dominates F, so G c-commands F.

3. General Rules for C-command

From this tree, we confirm the general principles of c-command:

① Sister nodes always c-command each other.
- B ↔ C, D ↔ E, F ↔ G.

② A node c-commands its sisters and their descendants.
- D c-commands E's descendants (F and G).
- E c-commands D.

③ A node does NOT c-command its ancestors or its mother.
- E does not c-command C or A.
- F does not c-command E, C, or A.

④ Nodes higher up in the tree have a broader c-command domain.
- C c-commands everything dominated by A except itself.
- E c-commands F and G, but not C or D.

4. Why C-command Matters

C-command is essential in explaining several key syntactic and semantic phenomena.

- Binding Theory (e.g., pronouns and reflexives)
  Example: "Himself likes John" is ungrammatical because "himself" must be c-commanded by its antecedent ("John").

- Quantifier Scope Ambiguity
  Example: "Everyone loves someone."
  Can mean:
  √ For every person, there exists someone they love.
  √ There is one particular person whom everyone loves.
  The interpretation depends on which NP c-commands the other.

- Negative Polarity Licensing
  Example: "I don't think anyone will come."
  The negative element "don't" must c-command the negative polarity item ("anyone") for the sentence to be grammatical.

C-command

Key Takeaways

- C-command is a crucial syntactic relationship that determines grammatical dependencies.
- A node c-commands its sisters and their descendants but not its mother or ancestors.
- C-command plays a key role in Binding Theory, Scope, and Negation.

Predicates, Arguments, and Thematic Roles

Predicates and Arguments

This section explains how verbs (predicates) and their required elements (arguments) work together to form meaningful sentences.

1. Why Do Some Sentences Sound Incomplete?

Look at these sentences

> The crocodile devoured a doughnut.
> *Devoured a doughnut. (Who did the action?)
> *The crocodile devoured. (Devoured what?)

The verb devour needs both a subject (who is doing the action) and an object (what is being devoured). Without these, the sentence is ungrammatical.

- A predicate is a word (usually a verb) that needs one or more participants (arguments) to form a complete sentence.
- Arguments are the necessary elements (subjects, objects) that complete the sentence's meaning.

2. How Many Arguments Does a Predicate Need?

Different predicates need different numbers of arguments

Sentence	Predicate (Verb)	Arguments	Predicate Type
Henry smiled.	smile	1 (subject)	One-place predicate (monadic)
The police investigated the case.	investigate	2 (subject + object)	Two-place predicate (dyadic)
Sara gave Pete a parcel.	give	3 (subject + indirect object + direct object)	Three-place predicate (triadic)
Melany bet Brian a pound that he would lose.	bet	4 (subject + indirect object + direct object + clause)	Four-place predicate

What Do These Mean?

- One-place predicates → The verb needs only one argument (subject).
  Example: smile (Henry smiled).

- Two-place predicates → The verb needs two arguments (subject + object).
  Example: investigate (The police investigated the case).

- Three-place predicates → The verb needs three arguments (subject + indirect object + direct object).
  Example: give (Sara gave Pete a parcel).

- Four-place predicates → The verb needs four arguments (subject + indirect object + direct object + a clause).
  Example: bet (Melany bet Brian a pound that he would lose).

3. Internal vs. External Arguments

- External argument → The subject of the sentence.
- Internal arguments → Objects, indirect objects, or complements that follow the verb.

Example:
Lisa gave John a book.

Lisa (external argument) → Subject.
John (internal argument) → Indirect object.
A book (internal argument) → Direct object.

Predicates and Arguments

4. How Linguists Represent Predicates and Arguments

Linguists use argument structure notation to show how many arguments a predicate takes.

Predicate	Structure
devour	[<u>1 <NP></u>, 2 <NP>]
smile	[<u>1 <NP></u>]
investigate	[<u>1 <NP></u>, 2 <NP>]
give	[<u>1 <NP></u>, 2 <NP>, 3 <NP>]
bet	[<u>1 <NP></u>, 2 <NP>, 3 <NP>, 4 <clause>]

- The first argument (subject) is underlined.
- The remaining arguments are objects or complements.
- Optional arguments (can be left out) are in parentheses.

Example of an Optional Argument

A: Ivan gave me a book for Christmas.
B: Ivan is so boring. He always gives books!

In B's sentence, the indirect object ("me") is missing, but the meaning is still understood.

5. Predicates Beyond Verbs: Nouns, Adjectives, and Prepositions

Predicates are not just verbs—they can also be nouns, adjectives, and prepositions.

Predicate Type	Example	Arguments
Noun Predicate	Paul's <u>study</u> of art history.	Paul (subject), art history (object)
Adjective Predicate	Freddy is <u>fond</u> of his sister.	Freddy (subject), his sister (object)
Prepositional Predicate	The bird is <u>inside</u> the house.	The bird (subject), the house (location)

- Noun predicates (e.g., study) require who is doing the action and what is being studied.
- Adjective predicates (e.g., fond) require who has the feeling and what the feeling is directed at.
- Prepositional predicates (e.g., inside) require who is being located and where they are.

Key Takeaways

- Predicates need arguments to form a meaningful sentence.
- Different predicates require different numbers of arguments:
    - Smile (1 argument) → Subject only
    - Investigate (2 arguments) → Subject + object
    - Give (3 arguments) → Subject + indirect object + direct object
    - Bet (4 arguments) → Subject + indirect object + direct object + clause
- Subjects are external arguments, while objects are internal arguments.
- Predicates aren't just verbs—they can also be nouns, adjectives, or prepositions.

Thematic Roles

1. What Are Thematic Roles?

Imagine a sentence as a mini-drama where each participant (argument) has a specific role to play. These roles are called thematic roles (or theta roles), and they describe how different participants relate to the action in a sentence.

Linguists do not fully agree on the exact number of thematic roles, but the following are widely accepted:

Thematic Role	Description	Example Sentence
Agent	The doer of the action (usually the subject).	The chef baked a cake.
Patient	The entity affected by the action.	The chef baked a cake.
Theme	The entity undergoing a process or being described.	The wind moved the leaves.
Experiencer	The entity experiencing a sensation or emotion.	Lisa loves chocolate.
Goal	The destination or endpoint of an action.	He walked to the store.
Source	The starting point of movement or transfer.	He came from Paris.
Benefactive	The entity benefiting from the action.	She baked a cake for her friend.
Instrument	The tool or means used to perform the action.	He wrote a letter with a pen.
Locative	The place where the action occurs.	She lives in Seoul.
Proposition	A statement or idea being expressed.	She believes that he is honest.

2. Thematic Roles and Argument Structures

Each predicate (verb) has a thematic structure, meaning it assigns specific thematic roles to its arguments.

Predicate	Thematic Structure
devour (verb)	[1 <NP, Agent>, 2 <NP, Patient>]
smile (verb)	[1 <NP, Agent>]
investigate (verb)	[1 <NP, Agent>, 2 <NP, Patient>]
give (verb)	[1 <NP, Agent>, (2 <NP, Benefactive>), 3 <NP, Theme>]
bet (verb)	[1 <NP, Agent>, 2 <NP, Goal>, 3 <NP, Patient>, 4 <clause, Proposition>]

- The first argument (Agent) is always the subject.
- Objects receive different roles depending on the verb.
- Optional arguments (like the Benefactive in "give") are in parentheses.

Thematic Roles

3. Non-Thematic Elements in Sentences

Some elements in a sentence do not receive thematic roles because they do not participate in the event.

① Dummy Subjects (Expletives)

Some subjects do not refer to real-world entities but only serve a grammatical function.

- Weather "it" (Expletive it)

It always rains in London.

It does not refer to anything; it just fills the subject position.

- Existential "there"

There were six policemen on the bus.

There does not refer to a location; it simply introduces existence.

Expletive 'it' and Existential 'there' are purely Subject slot fillers.

Then, compare these to real referential pronouns
- Referential "it"
   ⓐ I hate the number 31 bus. It is always packed!
- Locative "there"
   ⓑ Put your coffee over there.

In ⓐ and ⓑ, "it" and "there" refer to actual things, so they are not expletives.

② Adjuncts (Non-Arguments)

Adjuncts provide extra information but are NOT arguments.

Consider this modified sentence:

Last night, the crocodile greedily devoured a doughnut.

- Last night (time) and greedily (manner) do not participate in the event.
- They only add circumstantial details (when and how the action happened).
- Adjuncts are optional and can be removed without making the sentence ungrammatical.

Difference Between Arguments and Adjuncts

Feature	Argument	Adjunct
Essential to sentence meaning?	Yes	No
Can it be omitted?	No	Yes
Receives a thematic role?	Yes	No
Example	Lisa gave John a book. (John = argument)	Lisa gave John a book yesterday. (yesterday = adjunct)

Key Takeaways

- Thematic roles explain how arguments relate to the action in a sentence.
- Common thematic roles include Agent (doer), Patient (affected), Theme (undergoer), Experiencer (feeler), Goal (destination), and Source (origin).
- Each verb assigns specific thematic roles based on its argument structure.
- Not everything in a sentence is an argument:
  - Expletives ("it rains", "there is") do not refer to real things.
  - Adjuncts (time, manner, place expressions) just add extra details.

Grammatical Functions and Thematic Roles

1. Why Do We Need Thematic Roles?

Grammatical functions (like subject, object) and thematic roles (like Agent, Patient) are not the same.

A single noun phrase (NP) can have different grammatical functions in different sentences but still carry the same thematic role.

Let's analyze this through sentences with the verb 'smash.'
- David smashed the window.
- The window was smashed by David.
- A brick smashed the window.
- David used a brick to smash the window.

2. Thematic Roles vs. Grammatical Functions

Example Analysis

Sentence	Grammatical Function of NP	Thematic Role
David smashed the window.	David = Subject	Agent
	The window = Direct Object	Patient
The window was smashed by David.	The window = Subject	Patient
	David = Object of Preposition	Agent
A brick smashed the window.	A brick = Subject	Instrument
	The window = Direct Object	Patient
David used a brick to smash the window.	David = Subject	Agent
	A brick = Direct Object	Instrument
	The window = Direct Object (of smash)	Patient

3. Why This Distinction Matters

- Grammatical functions (subject, object, complement) = Syntactic category
- Thematic roles (Agent, Patient, Instrument, etc.) = Semantic role
- There is no one-to-one relationship between grammatical functions and thematic roles.
- This explains why
  · A Passive sentence still conveys the same thematic roles, even though the grammatical functions change.
  · The same NP can have different grammatical roles across sentences but still play the same semantic role in the event.

Key Takeaways

- Grammatical functions = Syntactic roles (Subject, Object, Complement).
- Thematic roles = Semantic roles (Agent, Patient, Instrument, etc.).
- One NP can change grammatical function but still have the same thematic role.
- Passive voice changes grammatical function but keeps the same thematic roles.
- Thematic roles help us understand sentence meaning beyond word order.

Further Thematic Relations

1. Why Thematic Roles Matter in Syntax
Thematic roles help explain why certain sentence structures behave similarly despite having different syntactic positions.

Transitive vs. Ergative Verbs

Consider the verb roll in the following sentences

ⓐ John rolled <u>the ball</u> down the hill.
ⓑ <u>The ball</u> rolled down the hill.

· In ⓐ, the ball is the Direct Object (Theme).
· In ⓑ, the ball is the Subject (Theme).

Key Insight
　• Even though the ball is a Direct Object in ⓐ and a Subject in ⓑ, it still has the same thematic role (Theme).
　• This shows that thematic roles remain constant even when syntactic structures change.

2. Thematic Roles and Syntactic Constraints

① Thematic Restrictions on Adverbs
Certain adverbs only work with specific thematic roles.

"Deliberately" only works with Agents
· John (Agent) deliberately rolled the ball down the hill.
· *The ball (Theme) deliberately rolled down the hill.

"Personally" only works with Experiencers
· Personally, I (Experiencer) don't like roses.
· Personally, your proposal doesn't interest me (Experiencer).
· *Personally, I (Agent) hit you.
· *Personally, you hit me (Theme).

② Thematic Constraints on Nominalization

Only Agentive verbs allow by-phrase nominalization

· The mayor (Agent) protested.
· The protest by the mayor.

· The mayor (Theme) died.
· *The death by the mayor.

Key Insight

- Protest allows a by-phrase because "protest" involves an Agent.
- Die does NOT allow a by-phrase because "die" involves a Theme, not an Agent.

③ Thematic Restrictions on Conjunctions

Only constituents with the same thematic role can be conjoined.

· John (Agent) broke the window.
· A hammer (Instrument) broke the window.
· *John and a hammer broke the window.

Key Insight

- John (Agent) and a hammer (Instrument) cannot be conjoined because they have different thematic roles.
- Only constituents with the same thematic role can be conjoined.

Subcategorization

1. What is Subcategorization?

Subcategorization refers to the specific grammatical requirements of a head word (e.g., a verb, noun, adjective, preposition, or adverb) regarding its complements. In simple terms, some words require specific types of phrases to follow them.

For example
- He destroyed the city.
- He destroyed. (Incorrect because "destroy" requires an object)

Key Idea: Different heads require different complements.

2. Subcategorization Frames

Subcategorization is represented using subcategorization frames, which specify what type of complement a word requires.

Example 1: The verb "destroy"
destroy (verb) → [— , NP]
- This means "destroy" must be followed by a noun phrase (NP).
- He destroyed the city.
- He destroyed. (Incorrect because NP is missing)

Example 2: The verb "send"
send (verb) → [— , NP NP]
- This means "send" requires two noun phrases (NPs) (e.g., an indirect and direct object).
- He sent her a letter.
- He sent. (Incorrect because NPs are missing)

Verbs with optional complements
send (verb) → [— , (NP) NP]
- The first NP (indirect object) is optional, so "He sent a letter." is also correct.

Example 3: The verb "blush" (intransitive verb)

blush (verb) → [—, 0]

- This means "blush" does not take a complement.
- He blushed.

3. Verbs That Allow Multiple Complement Types

Some verbs allow different complement structures.

Example: The verb "believe"

believe (verb) → [—, { NP | that-clause | to-infinitive clause }]

This means "believe" can be followed by one of three options

- Noun Phrase (NP): I believed the allegations.
- That-clause: I believed that the allegations were true.
- To-infinitive clause: I believed the allegations to be true.

4. Subcategorization Beyond Verbs

Subcategorization also applies to nouns, adjectives, prepositions, and adverbs.

Word Category	Example Word	Subcategorization Frame	Example Sentence
Noun	fact	[—, (that-clause)]	She hates the fact that he is a genius.
Adjective	appreciative	[—, of-NP]	She is appreciative of classical music.
Preposition	behind	[—, NP]	The bike is behind the shed.
Adverb	fortunately	[—, (for-NP)]	Fortunately for me, the train was late.

- Not only verbs but also nouns, adjectives, prepositions, and adverbs can specify what kind of complement follows them.

Subcategorization

Key Takeaways

- Subcategorization describes the types of complements a word requires.
- Each head word has a specific "subcategorization frame" that shows what it must be followed by.
- Some words require complements (e.g., "destroy" must have an object).
- Some words allow different types of complements (e.g., "believe" can take an NP, a that-clause, or a to-infinitive clause).
- Subcategorization applies not only to verbs but also to nouns, adjectives, prepositions, and adverbs.

Selectional Restrictions

1. What Are Selectional Restrictions?

Selectional restrictions refer to semantic limitations that predicates impose on their arguments. In simple terms, some words cannot logically combine with others because they violate real-world knowledge.

Consider These Sentences
ⓐ The keyboard designed some clothes.
ⓑ The stapler took a break.
ⓒ My colleague broke his feelings.

What's wrong with them?
ⓐ Problem: A keyboard is not animate, so it cannot "design" clothes.
ⓑ Problem: A stapler is not a living thing, so it cannot "take a break".
ⓒ Problem: "Feelings" are abstract, but "break" requires a concrete object.

Corrected Versions
ⓐ The designer designed some clothes. (Now the subject is animate!)
ⓑ My colleague took a break. (Now the subject is a person!)
ⓒ My colleague hurt his feelings. (Now the verb matches the object!)

2. How Selectional Restrictions Work

Linguists explain selectional restrictions using semantic features.

Feature Type	Meaning	Example of Correct Pairing	Example of Violation
[+animate]	The subject must be a living entity.	The designer created a dress.	The keyboard designed a dress.
[+human]	The subject must be a human.	The teacher explained the lesson.	The dog explained the lesson.
[+concrete]	The object must be a tangible thing.	She broke the glass.	She broke her feelings.
[+abstract]	The object must be an idea or concept.	She discussed the theory.	She discussed the table.

- A predicate (verb) carries specific features, and its arguments must match those features to form a meaningful sentence.

Selectional Restrictions

3. Why Selectional Restrictions Matter

- They help explain why some sentences feel "wrong" even if they are grammatically correct.
  - She ate an apple. (Correct)
  - *She ate an idea. (Ideas cannot be eaten!)
- They play a role in sentence processing and meaning interpretation.
  - When reading "The stapler took a break," we immediately recognize it as nonsensical.
- They influence how we teach language learning and machine translation.
  - Language learners (and AI systems) must learn these restrictions to avoid unnatural sentences.

Key Takeaways

- Selectional restrictions are semantic rules that limit how words combine.
- A predicate (verb) imposes specific requirements on its arguments.
- Words carry semantic features like [+animate] or [+concrete], and they must match.
- Some sentences are ungrammatical not because of syntax, but because of selectional violations.

X-Bar Theory

Heads, Complements, and Specifiers (X-Bar Syntax)

1. What Is X-Bar Theory?

X-Bar Theory is a universal structure that applies to all phrases in a language. It explains how words combine to form phrases using three key components

① Head   → The central, most important word in a phrase.
② Complement → The phrase that completes the meaning of the Head.
③ Specifier   → An optional element that modifies or clarifies the Head + Complement combination.

2. Identifying Heads, Complements, and Specifiers

Let's analyze the phrases in the following sentences

① The defendants denied the charge: they claim that they did [VP not destroy the garden]
② She proposed [NP an analysis of the sentence]
③ Jack is [AP so fond of coffee]
④ They are [PP quite in agreement]
⑤ My sister cycles [AdvP much faster than me]

Phrase Type	Head	Complement	Specifier
Verb Phrase (VP)	destroy	the garden	not
Noun Phrase (NP)	analysis	of the sentence	an
Adjective Phrase (AP)	fond	of coffee	so
Prepositional Phrase (PP)	in	agreement	quite
Adverbial Phrase (AdvP)	faster	than me	much

3. Structure of X-Bar Phrases

Every phrase follows the same hierarchical structure, regardless of category

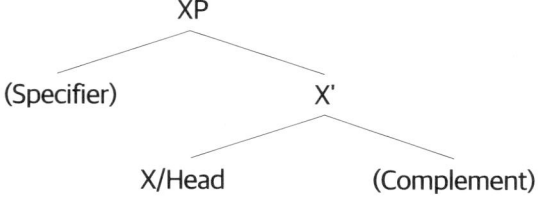

- XP (Phrase) → The entire phrase
- X' (X-bar) → An intermediate level between the Head and the full phrase
- X (Head) → The main word that determines the phrase type
- Complement → The phrase that completes the meaning of the Head
- Specifier → A modifier that applies to the Head + Complement

Example: VP Structure for "not destroy the garden"

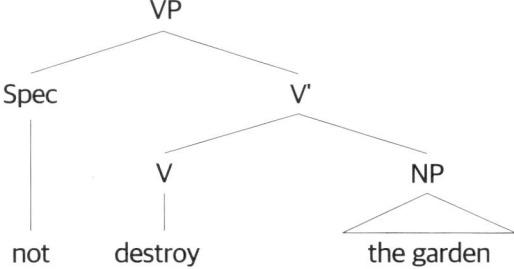

Example: NP Structure for "an analysis of the sentence"

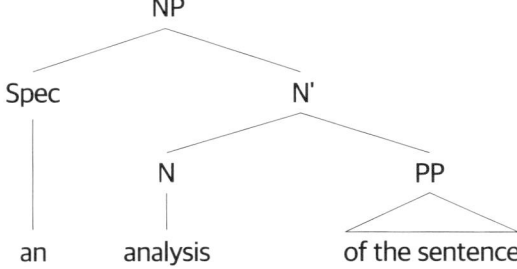

Heads, Complements, and Specifiers (X-Bar Syntax)

4. Why Is X-Bar Theory Important?

① It shows that all phrases have a consistent structure
NP, VP, AP, PP, and AdvP all follow the same pattern.

② It explains how Heads and Complements interact
"Destroy" requires an object (the garden), just like "fond" requires a complement (of coffee).

③ It accounts for optional Specifiers
Some phrases must have Complements (e.g., destroy the garden), but Specifiers are optional (e.g., so fond of coffee).

④ It provides a foundation for understanding sentence structure
X-Bar Theory is the basis for more advanced syntax models like Minimalism.

Adjuncts in X-Bar Theory

1. What Are Adjuncts?

So far, we have seen that phrases contain a Head, a Complement, and sometimes a Specifier. However, phrases can also contain Adjuncts, which provide extra, non-essential information.

Adjuncts answer questions like:
- How? (He walked slowly.)
- When? (She arrived after dinner.)
- Where? (They met in the park.)
- Why? (He left because of the rain.)

Adjuncts modify the meaning of the phrase but are not required for grammaticality.

Example:
The defendants denied the charge: they claim that they did [VP not destroy the garden deliberately].

- Head: destroy
- Complement: the garden (required for meaning)
- Specifier: not (modifies the verb phrase)
- Adjunct: deliberately (adds extra information about how the action was performed)

2. Adjuncts vs. Complements

Adjuncts and Complements both follow the Head, but their roles are different.

Feature	Complement	Adjunct
Required?	Yes (needed for meaning)	No (optional, adds detail)
Relationship with Head	Strong (directly related)	Weak (only modifies)
Position in Tree	Sister to Head (X)	Sister to X' (X-bar)

Adjuncts in X-Bar Theory

Example

- Correct Order of Complement & Adjunct
  She [VP read the book carefully].

  "the book" (Complement) must come right after the verb.
  "carefully" (Adjunct) comes after the Complement.

- Incorrect Order (Ungrammatical)
  *She read carefully the book.

Adjuncts cannot come between the Head and the Complement!

3. Adjunct Placement in Tree Diagrams
Adjuncts can be attached at different positions in the phrase structure

- Right-Adjunction (Post-Head Adjuncts)
[VP not destroy the garden deliberately].

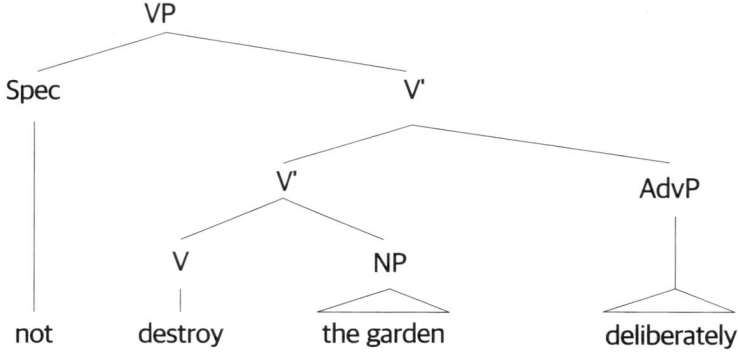

The Adjunct deliberately is added after the Complement the garden.

- Left-Adjunction (Pre-Head Adjuncts)

[VP not deliberately destroy the garden].

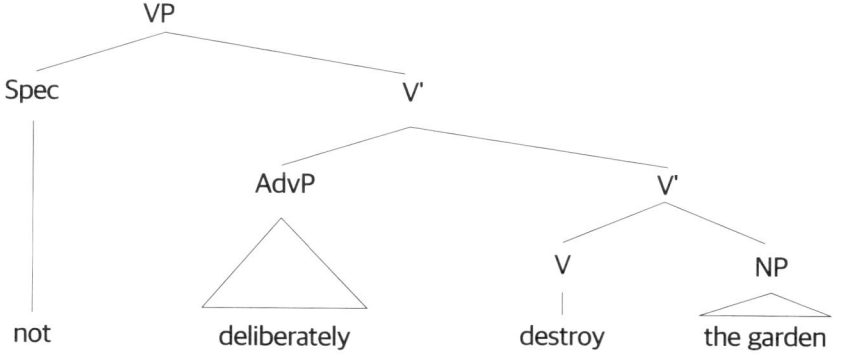

The Adjunct deliberately comes before the Head destroy.

Key Idea

- Adjuncts can be added on either side of X' (X-bar).
- Complements must be closer to the Head than Adjuncts.

4. Adjuncts in Different Phrase Types

Adjuncts are not limited to verb phrases (VPs). They can also appear in:

Phrase Type	Example Phrase	Adjunct
Noun Phrase (NP)	an analysis of the sentence with tree diagrams	with tree diagrams
Adjective Phrase (AP)	so fond of coffee after dinner	after dinner
Prepositional Phrase (PP)	quite in agreement about this	about this
Adverbial Phrase (AdvP)	much faster than me by far	by far

Adjuncts in X-Bar Theory

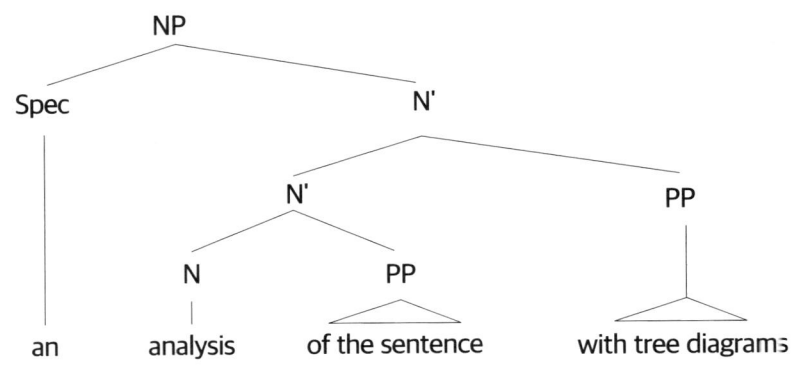

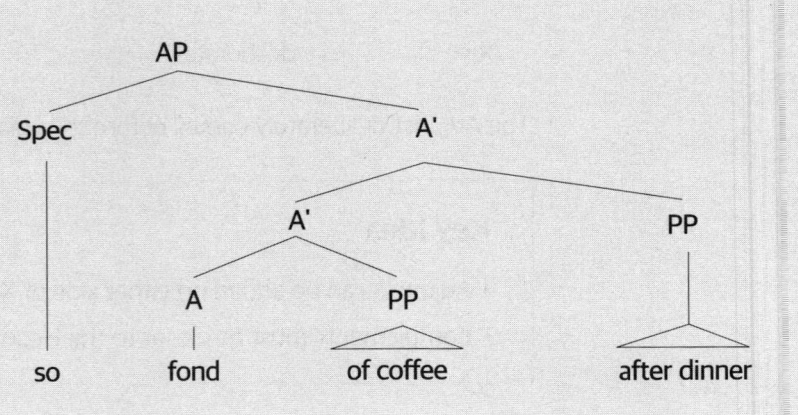

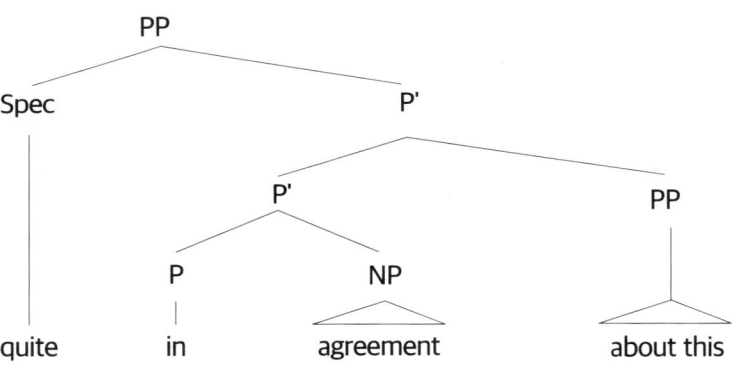

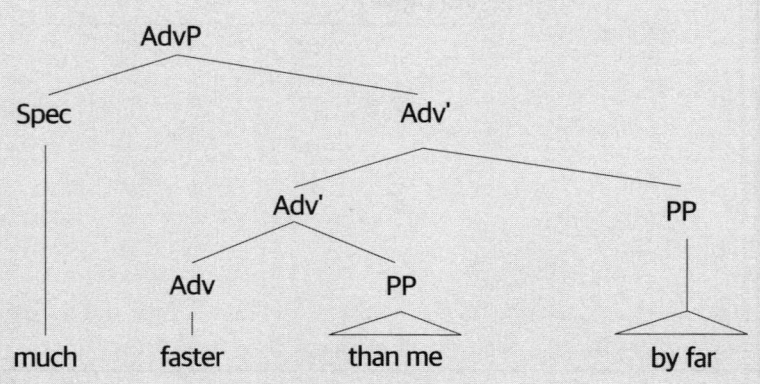

5. Stacking Adjuncts (Multiple Adjuncts in One Phrase)

Adjuncts can be stacked, meaning multiple Adjuncts can appear in one phrase:

- Example: VP with Multiple Adjuncts

The defendants denied the charge: they claim that they did [VP not unthinkingly, deliberately destroy the garden].

"unthinkingly" (first Adjunct)
"deliberately" (second Adjunct)

- Example: AP with Multiple Adjuncts

[AP so terribly fond of coffee after dinner].
"so terribly" (pre-Head Adjuncts)
"after dinner" (post-Head Adjunct)

Key Takeaways

- Adjuncts are optional modifiers that provide extra meaning (How? When? Where? Why?).
- Adjuncts attach to X' (X-bar), while Complements attach to X (Head).
- Adjuncts can appear before or after the Head but must be farther from the Head than Complements.
- Multiple Adjuncts can appear in one phrase.
- Adjuncts can appear in NPs, VPs, APs, PPs, and AdvPs.

Cross-Categorial Generalizations in X-Bar Syntax

1. What Is a Cross-Categorial Generalization?

A cross-categorial generalization means that all phrase types (NPs, VPs, APs, PPs, and AdvPs) share the same internal structure.

- Every phrase follows the same hierarchical structure, no matter its category.
- X-Bar Syntax (X') provides a universal framework for understanding phrase structure.

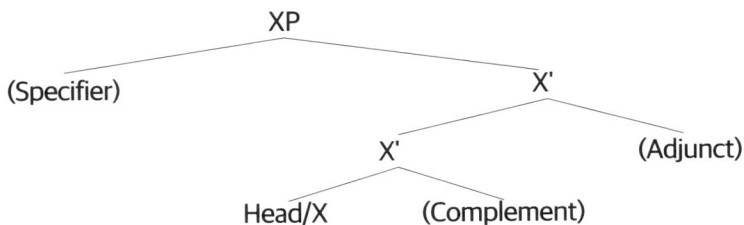

2. Why Is This Important?

① All phrases have the same fundamental structure.
- Whether it's a VP (destroy the garden), an NP (analysis of the sentence), or an AP (fond of coffee), the same X-bar hierarchy applies.

② The Head is the only required element in every phrase.
- A phrase cannot exist without a Head, but Specifiers, Complements, and Adjuncts are optional.

③ The existence of X' (X-bar) is justified syntactically.
- The intermediate level X' (X-bar) accounts for the structural separation between Complements and Adjuncts.
- Complements are always closer to the Head than Adjuncts.

Complements vs. Adjuncts: Extraposition (Postposing)

1. What Is Extraposition (Postposing)?

Extraposition (or postposing) refers to the movement of a phrase to the end of a clause.

2. The Difference in Movement Between Complements and Adjuncts

Let's compare two sentences where a Prepositional Phrase (PP) is moved:

- Adjunct PP (freely moved)

    A student came to see me yesterday [with long hair].
    - "With long hair" is extra descriptive information → it is an Adjunct.
    - The sentence is still grammatical after moving it.

- Complement PP (cannot be moved)

    *A student came to see me yesterday [of Physics].
    - "Of Physics" is necessary to complete the meaning → it is a Complement.
    - Moving it makes the sentence ungrammatical.

3. Why Are Complements More Resistant to Extraposition?

① Complements are tightly linked to the Head.
- They provide essential information about the Head.
- If moved, the sentence meaning becomes unclear or ungrammatical.

② Adjuncts are more flexible.
- They provide extra, non-essential details.
- If moved, the sentence remains grammatical.

Complements vs. Adjuncts: Preposing

1. What Is Preposing?
Preposing refers to moving a phrase to the front of a sentence for emphasis or question formation.

2. The Difference in Preposing Between Complements and Adjuncts
Consider the following examples

① Preposing a Complement (Grammatical)
[What branch of Physics] are you a student of?
- "Of Physics" is a Complement of "student".
- The Object of the Preposition (branch of Physics) can be moved to the front.
- The sentence remains grammatical.

② Preposing an Adjunct (Ungrammatical)
*[What kind of hair] are you a student with?
- "With long hair" is an Adjunct of "student".
- The Object of the Preposition (kind of hair) cannot be moved to the front.
- The sentence becomes ungrammatical.

3. Why Can Complements Be Preposed, but Not Adjuncts?
① Complements are tightly connected to the Head.
- They are essential for meaning, so moving them still preserves grammaticality.
- Prepositional Complements can be preposed without issue.

② Adjuncts are optional modifiers.
- They provide extra, non-essential details.
- Moving an Adjunct disrupts sentence structure, making it ungrammatical.

The Differences Between Complements and Adjuncts

1. Key Differences Between Complements and Adjuncts

Complements and Adjuncts both modify a noun, but they function differently. Here's an overview of their differences:

Rule	Complement	Adjunct
1. Semantic Nature	Necessary for meaning (defines the noun)	Optional, adds extra information
2. Ordering	Must appear closer to the noun	Appears after the complement
3. Stacking	Cannot be stacked	Can be stacked
4. Coordination	Can be coordinated only with other complements	Can be coordinated only with other adjuncts
5. Extraposition	Resists being moved to the end	Can be moved to the end
6. Preposing	Can be moved to the front in questions	Cannot be moved to the front

2. Explanation of the Rules

① Rule 1: Semantic Nature (Meaning Contribution)

Complements define the noun's essential meaning.
Adjuncts just provide extra, non-essential details.

Example
- A student [of Physics] (= Complement, specifies field of study)
- A student [with long hair] (= Adjunct, describes appearance)

② Rule 2: Ordering of Adjuncts and Complements

Complements must come closer to the noun.
Adjuncts must come after the complement.

Example
- Correct Order

The student [of Physics] [with long hair].
- Incorrect Order

*The student [with long hair] [of Physics].

The Differences Between Complements and Adjuncts

③ Rule 3: Stacking (Multiple Modifiers in a Row)
Adjuncts can be stacked freely (recursive rule).
Complements cannot be stacked (non-recursive).

- Example: Adjuncts can stack

The student [with long hair] [with short arms].

- Example: Complements cannot stack

*The student [of Physics] [of Chemistry].

④ Rule 4: Coordination (Joining with 'and')
Two complements can be coordinated.
Two adjuncts can be coordinated.
A complement and an adjunct cannot be coordinated.

- Correct Coordination Examples

A student [of Physics] and [of Chemistry]. (Complement + Complement)
A student [with long hair] and [with short arms]. (Adjunct + Adjunct)

- Incorrect Coordination Examples

*A student [of Physics] and [with long hair].
*A student [with long hair] and [of Physics].

Why?
- Complements attach to the noun (N-level).
- Adjuncts attach higher up (N-bar level).
- Only elements at the same level can be coordinated.

⑤ Rule 5: Extraposition (Postposing to the End)
Adjuncts can move more freely to the end of a clause.
Complements resist being moved.

- Example: Adjunct Moves Easily

A student ___ came to see me yesterday [with long hair].

- Example: Complement Cannot Be Moved

*A student ___ came to see me yesterday [of Physics].

Why?
- Complements are too closely linked to the noun.
- Adjuncts are more loosely connected, so they can move.

⑥ Rule 6: Preposing (Fronting for Questions)
Complements can be preposed easily.
Adjuncts resist preposing.

- Example: Complement Preposed Correctly

[What branch of Physics] are you a student of?

- Example: Adjunct Cannot Be Preposed

*[What kind of hair] are you a student with?

Why?
- Complements are part of the core meaning of the noun, so they can be questioned and moved.
- Adjuncts are loosely connected, so moving them creates an unnatural structure.

Clauses & Movement

The I-node (Inflectional Node)

1. What Is the I-node?

The I-node (Inflectional Node) is a syntactic category that plays a crucial role in sentence structure.

It is responsible for:

① Assigning tense to verbs (e.g., past, present, future).
② Ensuring subject-verb agreement (e.g., "he bakes" vs. "they bake").
③ Housing auxiliary verbs like modals (e.g., "will," "can").
④ Containing the infinitival marker "to" in nonfinite clauses.

2. Basic Sentence Structure With the I-node

Consider the simple sentence

- My brother baked a cake.

Before introducing the I-node, we might structure this as:

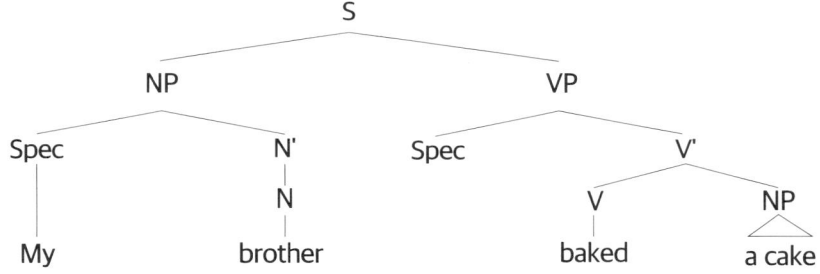

However, this does not account for tense and agreement.

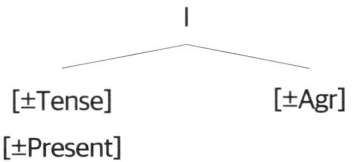

[±Tense]
[±Present]   [±Agr]

The I-node (Inflectional Node)

To fix this, we introduce I (Inflection) between NP and VP:

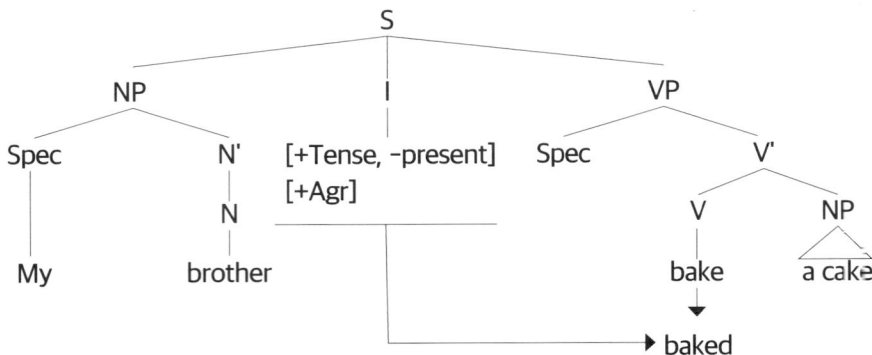

The I-node assigns past tense (-ed) to "bake" and ensures subject-verb agreement.(Affix Hopping)

3. Finite vs. Nonfinite Clauses in the I-node
A clause can be finite or nonfinite.

Finite Clause Example
She wanted [her brother to bake a cake].
- "wanted" is finite (past tense, agrees with "she").
- "to bake" is nonfinite (has no tense).

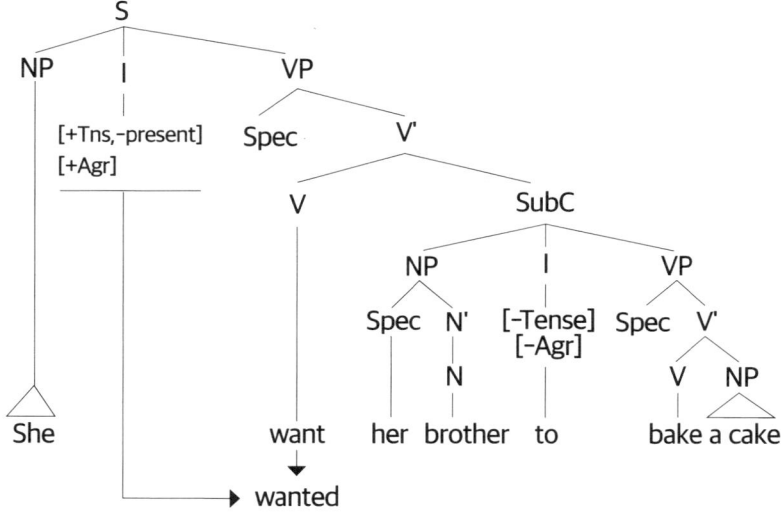

4. The Role of Modals in the I-node

Consider the example with a Modal:

My brother will bake a cake.

At first, we might assume that "will" is inside the VP, as it is a verb. However, this assumption creates structural issues, especially when negation ("not") is introduced.

My brother will not bake a cake.

- "Not" appears between "will" and "bake."
- If "will" were inside VP, there would be no structural position available for "not" to intervene.

This observation suggests that modal auxiliaries like "will" are not inside the VP but instead belong to the I-node.

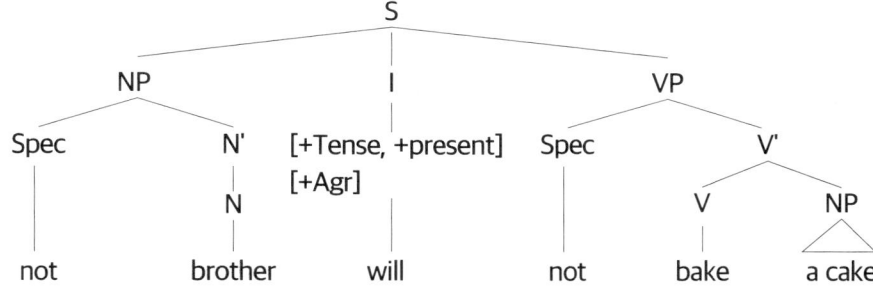

The I-node (Inflectional Node)

5. Sentence Adverbs as Evidence for the I-node

Sentence adverbs (e.g., perhaps, probably, frankly, however, definitely, certainly) modify entire sentences and provide evidence that modals belong under I.

Example
My brother will probably not bake a cake.

Possible Adverb Placements
① Perhaps my brother will not bake a cake.
② My brother perhaps will not bake a cake.
③ My brother will perhaps not bake a cake.
④ My brother will not bake a cake perhaps.

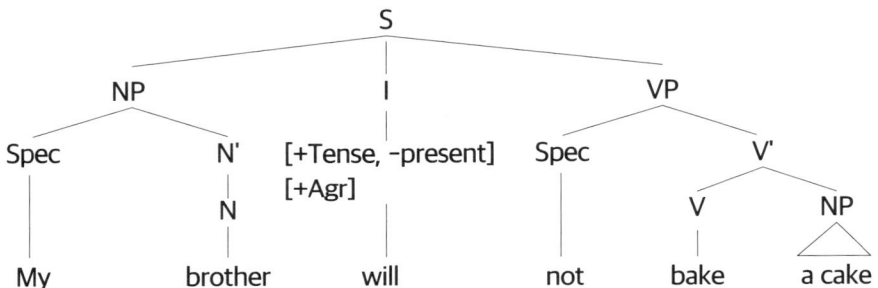

Affix Movement vs. V Movement

In syntactic theory, one major question is how tense and agreement features from the I-node (Inflection) end up attached to a verb that originally appears as the head (V) of VP. There are two competing explanations for this process:
Affix Movement and V Movement (V-to-I Movement).

1. Affix Movement

One approach suggests that tense and agreement features from I attach to the verb without any movement of the verb itself. This is called Affix Movement.

Consider the sentence
John annoys me.

Here, the verb annoy acquires the third-person singular -s from I, resulting in the inflected verb annoys, but the verb itself remains in V of VP

John   [I e]   [vp   [v   annoy]   me]

John   [vp   [v   annoys]   me]

According to this theory, the tense and agreement affix is simply transferred from I onto the verb in V of VP, with no structural movement.

Affix Movement vs. V Movement

2. V Movement (V-to-I Movement)

A different theory argues that the verb itself moves from V of VP to I when there is no modal verb occupying I. This movement is called V-to-I Movement, where the verb moves up to I and acquires tense/agreement features.

The same sentence under this analysis looks like

John   [₁ e]   [vp   [v annoy]   me]

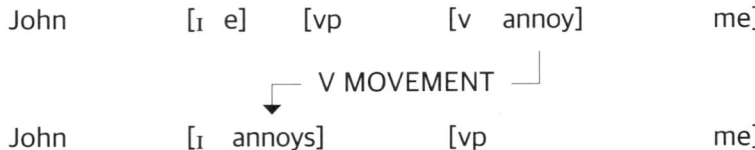

John   [₁ annoys]   [vp   me]

Here, the verb annoy moves from V of VP into I, rather than remaining inside VP. The difference between the two theories is that in Affix Movement, the verb stays in V of VP, whereas in V-to-I Movement, the verb moves into I.

The question now is: which of these analyses is correct?
To determine this, we examine V Movement Analysis more closely.

3. V Movement Analysis

The V Movement argues that verbs move to I only when I is finite and empty. This explains why modals like will and can do not require verb movement—they already occupy I.

Consider the following example:
He has no money.

In the sentence, the verbs has does not remain in their original position inside the head of VP. Instead, they move to the I-node, which contains the sentence's tense and agreement features.

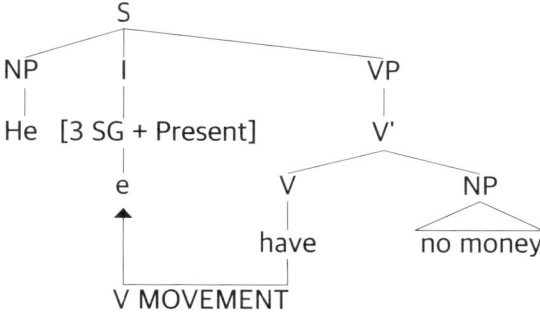

Here, the verb have moves from the V position inside VP to the I-node to receive tense marking, surfacing as has in the present tense.

① Negation and Verb Movement
Negation in English interacts with V movement in interesting ways.

Consider the following examples
- He may not have finished.
- He may not be working.

In these sentences:
- The modal verb may remains in the I position.
- The negation not appears after the modal and before the aspectual auxiliaries (have and be).

Affix Movement vs. V Movement

However, in sentences where have or be move to I, the negation follows the moved verb:

- He has not finished.
- He is not working.

Here, have and be move from VP to I, positioning them before negation.

This can be represented as follows:

He   [₁ e]   not   [vp have finished]

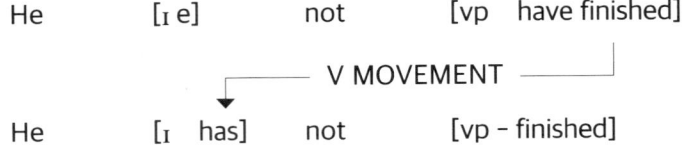

He   [₁ has]   not   [vp - finished]

② Adverb Distribution and V Movement

Adverb placement provides further evidence for V movement. In English, sentence adverbs like probably, certainly, and definitely can only appear in specific positions.

Consider:
ⓐ George will probably have been working.
ⓑ * George will have probably been working.
ⓒ * George will have been probably working.

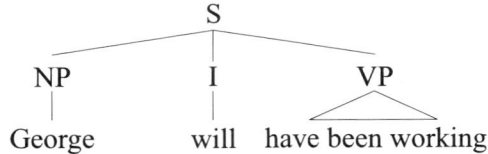

The grammatical sentence ⓐ shows that adverbs like probably occur before the auxiliary verbs inside VP but after modals.

③ Interaction with Modals and Aspectual Auxiliaries

V movement does not occur if I is already occupied by a modal verb, such as will:

- He has probably broken the mirror.
- I am probably dreaming.

Here, has and am must have moved to I because they appear before the adverb. This movement ensures that they acquire tense and agreement features.

However, consider:
He will not have broken the mirror.

In this sentence:
- The modal will occupies I, preventing have from moving to I.
- The auxiliary have remains inside VP, positioned after not.

The tree structure for this is:

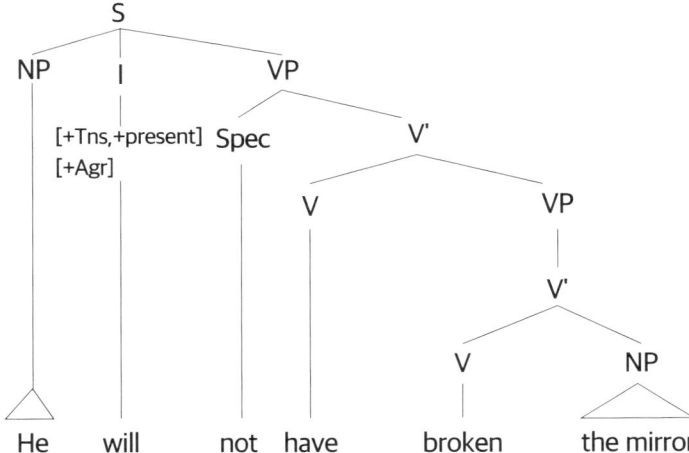

Since modals block V movement, have stays inside VP.

I Movement (I-to-C Movement)

I Movement, also known as I-to-C Movement, is a syntactic process that explains Subject-Auxiliary Inversion in English. This movement is essential for forming yes/no questions and is a core concept in generative grammar.

1. Subject-Auxiliary Inversion in Statements vs. Questions

Compare the following sentences

① Declarative sentence (statement)
- He will tell the truth.
- Structure: [S He [I will] [VP tell the truth]]

② Interrogative sentence (question)
- Will he tell the truth?
- Structure: [C Will] [S he [I -] [VP tell the truth]]

2. Explanation of the Process

In a statement, the auxiliary modal verb (will) is positioned inside the Inflectional Phrase (I) and follows the subject (he).

When forming a question, will moves to the Complementizer (C) position leaving behind a gap in I.

This process is known as I-to-C Movement and is schematized as follows:
- Deep Structure (before movement)

[C e] [S he [I will] [VP tell the truth]]

Here, "will" originates in I.

- Surface Structure (after movement)

[C Will] [S he [I -] [VP tell the truth]]

"Will" moves from I to C, creating the question form.

[c e]   [s he   [I will]   [vp tell the truth]]
         ┌─── I MOVEMENT ───┘
[c Will]   [s he   [I -]   [vp tell the truth]]?

3. Key Assumptions of I Movement

The analysis of I movement is based on two main assumptions:

① Modals originate in I.
- In statements, modal verbs (will, can, should) remain inside I.

② Modals move to C in questions.
- In questions, the modal moves from I to C, resulting in Subject-Auxiliary Inversion.

4. The Gap Argument

Consider the ungrammatical examples below:

- * Will [S he [I can] tell the truth]?
- * Will [S he [I to] tell the truth]?

Why are these sentences incorrect?
- The original I position was already occupied by "will" before moving to C.
- After "will" moves to C, a gap is left behind in I.
- However, the gap cannot be refilled with another modal (can) or infinitive marker(to).

This violates the "no refilling" condition: once a position has been filled, it cannot be refilled.

5. Have Contraction and I Movement

The contraction of "have" (to 've) depends on two conditions:

① The pronoun before "have" must end in a vowel or diphthong
Example: I've, you've, they've

② There must be no "gap" between the pronoun and "have".
If I movement creates a gap, contraction is blocked.

I Movement (I-to-C Movement)

Blocked contraction in questions

- Could they have/* they've done something to help?
- Would you have/* you've wanted to come with me?
- Should I have/* I've called the police?
- Will we have/* we've finished by 4 o'clock?

In these cases, I movement creates a gap (Ø) between the pronoun and have, preventing contraction.

Contrast with declaratives (no movement, contraction possible)

- I should have called the police.
- We will have finished by 4 o'clock.
- You would have wanted to come with me.
- They could have done something to help.

6. The Final Structure of I Movement

Having established that modals originate in I, we now determine where they move.

In yes/no questions, modals in I move to an empty C, as shown in the tree diagram:

- Deep Structure

[S He [I will] [VP tell the truth]]

- Surface Structure (after I-to-C movement)

[C Will] [S he [I -] [VP tell the truth]]

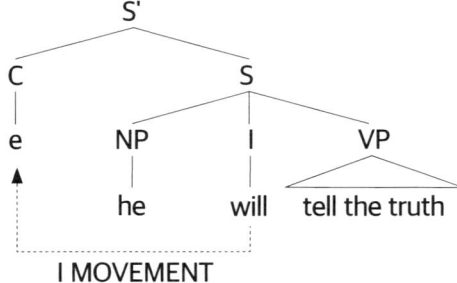

Trace

1. WANNA Contraction

In colloquial English, 'want to' can contract to 'wanna', as in:

①
ⓐ I want to win.
ⓑ I wanna win.

This contraction is also possible in WH-questions:

②
ⓐ Who do you want to beat ___?
ⓑ Who do you wanna beat?

However, wanna contraction is not always possible:

③
ⓐ Who do you want ___ to win?
ⓑ * Who do you wanna win?

· The difference between ② and ③ is due to a trace (or a gap) left behind by WH-movement.
· In ②, who is the object of beat, so there is no gap between want and to.
· But in ③, who is the subject of the embedded verb win, so it leaves a trace between want and to. This intervening trace blocks the contraction of want to into wanna.

Thus, wanna contraction is only allowed when there is no trace between want and to. This supports the idea that an underlying syntactic structure (Deep Structure) affects the surface form of a sentence.

Trace

2. HAVE Contraction

The auxiliary have can contract to /v/ (as in I've, we've, etc.) only under certain conditions:

- The pronoun must end in a vowel or diphthong.
- There must be no gap between the pronoun and have.

Consider these sentences:

①
ⓐ Should I have / *I've called the police?
ⓑ Will we have / *we've finished by 4 o'clock?
ⓒ Would you have / *you've wanted to come with me?
ⓓ Could they have / *they've done something to help?

Why is contraction blocked in these cases?
It is because of subject-auxiliary inversion in questions. In each sentence, the modal (should, will, would, could) originally appears after the subject in declarative sentences:

②
ⓐ I should have called the police.
ⓑ We will have finished by 4 o'clock.
ⓒ You would have wanted to come with me.
ⓓ They could have done something to help.

But in questions, the modal moves to the front (I-movement), leaving a gap (symbolized as Ø) between the pronoun and have:

③
ⓐ Should I Ø have called the police?
ⓑ Will we Ø have finished by 4 o'clock?
ⓒ Would you Ø have wanted to come with me?
ⓓ Could they Ø have done something to help?

This gap blocks the contraction of have. So, the sentence 'Should I've called the police?' is ungrammatical due to the trace left by movement.

Trace

In summary,
- both wanna and have contraction provide evidence for the existence of traces in
- syntax.
- Traces are the invisible positions left behind when elements move, and they can
- block certain phonological processes like contraction.
- Understanding traces helps us better grasp the relationship between deep and surface structures in syntax.

Wh-Movement

1. What is Wh-Movement?

Wh-Movement is a syntactic process in which wh-words (what, who, where, when, why, how) move from their original position in a sentence to the beginning, forming wh-questions.

Example
① Declarative sentence (no movement)
- You will buy what?

Structure: [S You [I will] [VP buy what]]

② Interrogative sentence (with Wh-Movement)
- What will you buy?

Structure: [C What] [C will] [S you [VP buy -]]

The wh-word (what) moves from the Direct Object (DO) position to the beginning of the sentence.

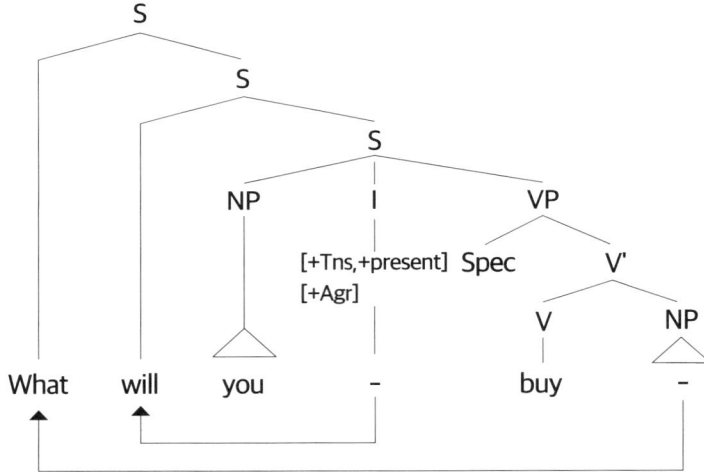

> Step-by-Step Transformation
>
> ① Deep Structure (before movement)
> You will buy what?
> [S You [I will] [VP buy what]]
>
> ② Wh-Movement applies:
> The wh-word what moves from DO position to Specifier of CP (C-Specifier).
> Simultaneously, I-to-C Movement applies, moving will to C.
>
> ③ Surface Structure (after movement)
> What will you buy?
> [CP What [C will] [S you [VP buy -]]]
> The trace (-) marks the original position of what, which is now empty.

2. Evidence for Wh-Movement

We can confirm that what originally belonged to the Direct Object position by considering a sentence where it remains in place:

You will buy WHAT?

Here, what occurs in its original DO position after buy.

This confirms that in "What will you buy?", the wh-word has moved from the DO position to the beginning.

Wh-Movement

3. The Tree Structure for Wh-Movement

Below is the syntactic structure of:

What will he do?

① Step 1: Original Sentence (Deep Structure)
He will do what?
[S He [I will] [VP do what]]

② Step 2: Applying I-to-C Movement
The modal will moves from I to C.
[CP [C will] [S he [VP do what]]

③ Step 3: Applying Wh-Movement
The wh-word what moves from the DO position to C-Specifier.

④ Final Surface Structure:
[CP What [C will] [S he [VP do -]]]

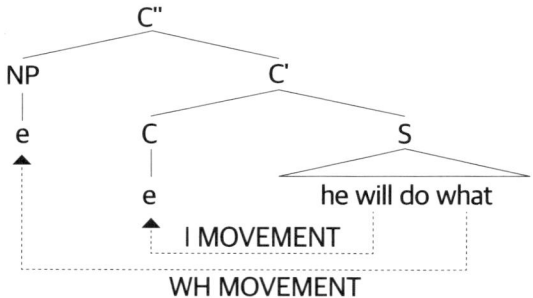

4. Understanding the CP Structure

The final surface structure follows the Complementizer Phrase (CP) format, which is equivalent to S' (S-bar) in traditional grammar.

The syntactic tree can be represented as:

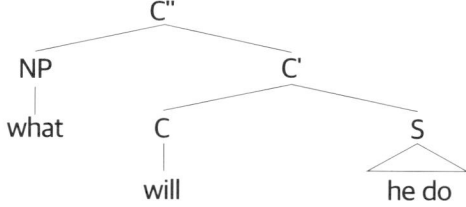

- What moves to Specifier of CP (C-Specifier).
- Will moves from I to C (I-to-C Movement).
- Trace (-) marks the original position of what.

NP-Movement in Passive

1. What is NP-Movement in Passive Sentences?

NP-Movement is a syntactic process where the Direct Object (DO) of an active sentence moves to the Subject position in a passive sentence.

For example

① Active sentence
- These lorries produce filthy fumes.

[S These lorries] [VP produce [NP filthy fumes]]

② Passive sentence
- Filthy fumes are produced by these lorries.

[S Filthy fumes] [VP are produced [by these lorries]]

Here, filthy fumes moves from the post-verbal object position in the active structure to the pre-verbal subject position in the passive structure.

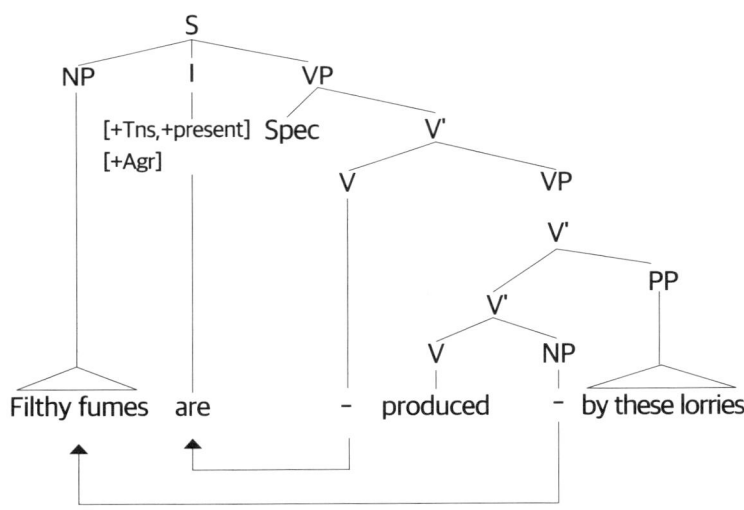

2. Key Properties of Passive Sentences

Passive constructions contain

- The passive auxiliary (be)
- A past participle form of the verb (produced)
- An optional "by-phrase" indicating the agent (by these lorries)

3. Why Does NP-Movement Happen?

The Agent (these lorries) remains the same in both the active and passive sentences, but the Theme/Patient (filthy fumes) moves to the Subject position. This movement allows passive structures to maintain the same thematic relationships while altering grammatical roles.

4. Evidence for NP-Movement in Passive Sentences

Linguists support the NP-Movement analysis using various syntactic arguments

① The Subcategorization Argument

Certain verbs require both an NP (object) and a PP (prepositional phrase). This subcategorization rule holds in active sentences, but passive sentences appear to violate it.

- Active sentence (subcategorization rule is followed)

John will put the car in the garage.

[S John] [VP will put [NP the car] [PP in the garage]]

- Passive sentence (surface violation of subcategorization)

The car will be put — in the garage.

[S The car] [VP will be put [PP in the garage]]

If put must always take both an NP and a PP, why is the passive version (The car will be put in the garage) grammatical?

The missing NP was originally there but moved to the Subject position. The deep structure still respects the subcategorization rule.

NP-Movement in Passive

② The Gap Argument

If NP-Movement occurs, we should expect that the original object position cannot be filled again by another NP.

- Passive sentence with a gap (grammatical)

The car will be put — in the garage.

- Passive sentence with another NP in the gap (ungrammatical)

* The car will be put the bike in the garage.

Why? The movement leaves a trace (gap), which cannot be refilled by another NP.

- Deep structure before movement

[S — will be put [NP the car] [PP in the garage]]

- Surface structure after movement

[S The car will be put — [PP in the garage]]

This supports the claim that the NP originally belonged in the object position and was moved.

③ Thematic Role Preservation

In active sentences, the Direct Object plays the role of Theme/Patient.
In passive sentences, the Subject still plays the role of Theme/Patient.

- Example with Theme/Patient Role

They rolled the ball down the hill. (Theme = the ball)
The ball was rolled down the hill. (Theme = the ball)

- Example with Goal Role

They will give Mary nothing. (Goal = Mary)
Mary will be given nothing. (Goal = Mary)

The thematic role remains the same, but the syntactic position changes.
This suggests that NPs move from object position to subject position in passive structures while maintaining their thematic roles.

④ Object Idiom Chunks Argument

Certain fixed expressions (idiom chunks) are only grammatical when they immediately follow specific verbs in their deep structure.

- Idiomatic expressions in active sentences

He pays heed to warnings.

The government keeps tabs on his operations.

She took note of what I said.

- Idiomatic expressions in passive sentences

Heed was paid — to warnings.

Tabs were kept — on his operations.

Note was taken — of what I said.

These expressions are only allowed in sentences where they follow their specific verbs.

However, in passive sentences, they appear before the verb, even though they still maintain their idiomatic meaning.

Why?

If NP-Movement did not occur, these idiom chunks should become ungrammatical when moved.

Since they remain grammatical, we conclude that they originated in the object position and then moved to subject position.

NP-Movement: Subject-to-Subject Raising

1. What is NP-Movement in Subject-to-Subject Raising?

NP-Movement (Subject-to-Subject Raising) is a syntactic phenomenon where a subject NP moves from the subordinate clause to the subject position of the main clause.

Consider the following sentences
ⓐ Danny seems to be working.
ⓑ Phil appears to be singing.

These sentences appear to have only one clause, but when we analyze them semantically, we realize that they actually involve two clauses.

- Sentence ⓐ can be paraphrased as:
It seems that Danny is working.

- Sentence ⓑ can be paraphrased as:
It appears that Phil is singing.

In these paraphrases, the dummy pronoun "it" takes the subject position in the matrix clause. However, in the original sentences, Danny and Phil are in the main clause subject position, even though their meaning belongs to the embedded clause.

2. How Does NP-Movement Work in Subject-to-Subject Raising?

Linguists explain that Danny and Phil do not receive their thematic roles from "seem" and "appear" but rather from the verbs in the subordinate clause ("working" and "singing").

We assume that
- Danny and Phil originally start in the subject position of the subordinate clause.
- They then move to the subject position of the main clause because "seem" and "appear" do not assign thematic roles to their subjects.

This results in the NP moving from the lower clause (subordinate) to the higher clause (matrix), which is why this process is called Subject-to-Subject Raising.

3. Syntactic Structure of Subject-to-Subject Raising

The deep structure of ⓐ and ⓑ would be

- Deep Structure Representation

(Danny) seems [Danny to be working].
(Phil) appears [Phil to be singing].

Since Danny and Phil receive their thematic roles from working and singing in the embedded clause, they should ideally remain there. However, due to the properties of "seem" and "appear", they must move to the subject position of the matrix clause.

This gives us the surface structure

- Surface Structure Representation

Danny seems to be working.
Phil appears to be singing.

Thus, the NP has moved from the embedded clause (to be working / to be singing) into the main clause subject position.

[$_{MC}$ Danny Seems [$_{subC}$ – to be working]]

[$_{MC}$ Phil appears [$_{subC}$ – to be singing]]

NP-Movement: Subject-to-Subject Raising

4. Why Does NP-Movement Occur?

The main verbs "seem" and "appear" are linking verbs, which means:

① They do not assign thematic roles to their subjects.

② They take clausal complements (entire clauses as arguments).

③ The actual thematic role is assigned in the embedded clause, not in the matrix clause.

The fact that we can paraphrase these sentences with a dummy pronoun ("it")

- It seems that Danny is working.
- It appears that Phil is singing.

suggests that the real subject is inside the lower clause and has been raised to the main clause.

5. Tree Diagram Representation

The movement of Danny and Phil can be represented as follows:

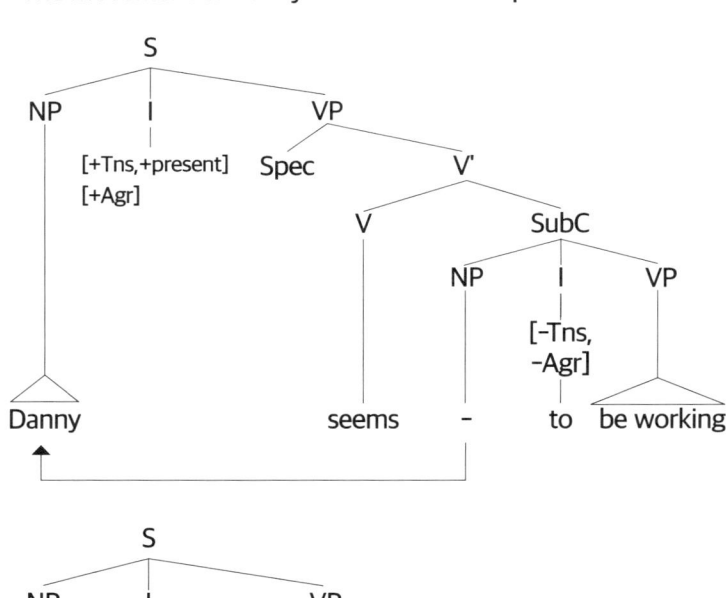

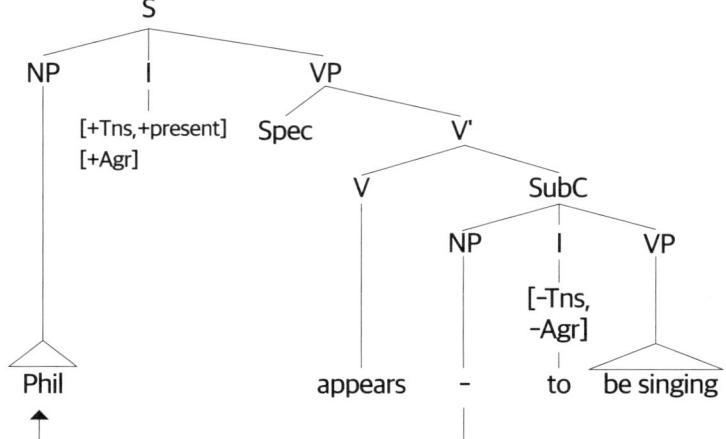

Constituency Tests

Constituency

1. What are Constituents?
Constituents are groups of words that function as syntactic and semantic units.

Constituency is formally defined in terms of dominance in tree structures:
- X dominates Y → Y is a constituent of X if X includes Y.
- X immediately dominates Y → Y is an immediate constituent of X if X s directly above Y in the tree structure.

2. Constituency Tests
To determine whether a group of words forms a constituent, several tests are used

① Movement Test
- Topicalization: Moving a phrase to the beginning of a sentence.
- Heavy NP Shift: Moving a long noun phrase to the end of the sentence.
- Extraposition of Subject Clauses: Moving a subject clause to the right.
- Extraposition from NP: Moving a clause out of a noun phrase.

② Substitution Test
- Proform Substitution: Replacing a phrase with a pronoun or auxiliary.
- NP-Substitution & N'-Substitution: Replacing noun phrases.
- VP-Substitution & V'-Substitution/Deletion: Replacing or deleting verb phrases.

③ Coordination Test
- Ordinary Coordination: Combining phrases using and or or.
- Shared Constituent Coordination: A shared constituent remains grammatically correct.

④ Cleft and Pseudocleft Test
- Cleft Test: Restructuring the sentence using It is/was X that....
- Pseudocleft Test: Using a relative clause (What X did was...).

⑤ Insertion Test
- Inserting words into a sentence to test constituency.

⑥ Constituent Response Test
- Checking if a phrase can serve as a stand-alone response to a question.

The Movement Test

Linguists use the Movement Test to determine whether a string of words behaves as a constituent by attempting to move it to a different position in a sentence. If movement is possible without causing ungrammaticality, the string is confirmed as a constituent.

1. Topicalization: Moving Constituents to the Left

Topicalization involves moving a constituent (such as a noun phrase, adjective phrase, prepositional phrase, or verb phrase) to the beginning of a sentence for emphasis.

- Direct Object Movement

Normal Order: I like Belgian beer but hate Belgian wine.

Topicalized: Belgian beer, I like, but Belgian wine, I hate.

- Noun Phrase (NP) Movement

Normal Order: I can't stand your elder sister.

Topicalized: Your elder sister, I can't stand.

Ungrammatical Cases (Moving Part of the NP):
* Elder sister, I can't stand your.
* Your, I can't stand elder sister.

- Other Phrases that Can Be Topicalized

Adjective Phrase (AP): Neurotic, I would say she is, not nervous.
Prepositional Phrase (PP): In his attic, he keeps his plants, not his pets.
Verb Phrase (VP): Write an essay, he will.

Principle

If a phrase headed by X (where X is N, A, P, or V) can be topicalized, it is an XP-constituent.

VP-Topicalization (VP-Preposing): Moving Verb Phrases to the Left

VP-Preposing is a syntactic movement process in which a verb phrase (VP) is moved to the beginning of a clause. This type of movement is a special case of Topicalization, applied specifically to VPs.

1. Evidence That VP is a Constituent

In VP-Preposing, a verb and its direct object move together, proving that they form a constituent (a VP).

- Normal Order: Ralph says that he will clean his room.
- VP-Preposing: Clean his room, he will.

Here, the VP ("clean his room") moves from its original position after "will" to the beginning of the clause. Since this movement is only possible for constituents, we confirm that "clean his room" forms a VP constituent.

2. VP-Preposing and Direct Objects

A VP must move as a whole, including both the verb and its direct object. We cannot move only the verb and leave the direct object behind.

Correct VP Movement
- Sally says that she will return my book, and [return my book] she will.
- Drew says that he will wash the dishes, and [wash the dishes] he will.

Ungrammatical (Leaving the Direct Object Behind)
* Ralph says that he will clean his room, and [clean] he will his room.
* Sally says that she will return my book, and [return] she will my book.
* Drew says that he will wash the dishes, and [wash] he will the dishes.

Conclusion
- The Direct Object cannot be separated from the verb during VP-Preposing.
- This supports the VP structure, where the Direct Object is a sister to the verb inside the VP.

3. VP-Preposing and Auxiliary Verbs

A key property of VP-Preposing is that it only applies if an auxiliary verb is present (e.g., will, did).

Sally said that she returned my book, and [return my book] she did.
* Sally said that she returned my book, and [returned my book] she.

- Modal and auxiliary verbs do not move during VP-Preposing.
- This shows that auxiliaries (will, did) are not part of the VP.
- If auxiliaries were part of the VP, they would move with it, but they stay behind.

Ralph says that he will clean his room, and [clean his room] he will.
* Ralph says that he will clean his room, and [will clean his room] he.

Conclusion
- Auxiliary verbs are separate from VP.
- Only the VP moves, leaving the auxiliary behind.

4. VP-Preposing and Adverb Phrases

Another test for VP constituency involves adverb phrases (AdvPs).

Ralph says that he will clean his room meticulously.

We apply VP-Preposing:
Clean his room meticulously, he will.
* Clean his room, he will meticulously.

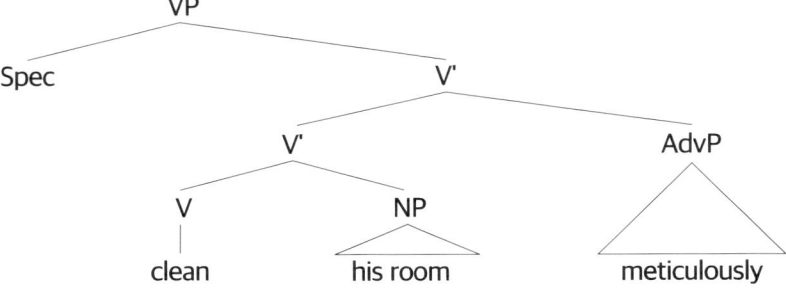

Heavy-NP-Shift: Moving Heavy Noun Phrases to the Right

Heavy-NP-Shift (HNPS) is a syntactic movement process in which long (or "heavy") noun phrases (NPs) move to the right of the sentence, away from their typical position.

1. Heavy NPs and Rightward Movement

In English, the default position of a Direct Object (DO) is immediately after the verb. However, when a Direct Object is "heavy" (i.e., long or complex), it can shift to the end of the sentence.

- Without HNPS

We brought six boxes of excellent French wine into the country.
She sold the prints that she had made at the market.

- With HNPS (NP moved right)

We brought — into the country six boxes of excellent French wine.
She sold — at the market the prints that she had made.

What triggers HNPS?
The NP is long or complex, containing additional modifiers such as:
· Prepositional Phrases (PPs): six boxes of excellent French wine
· Relative Clauses: the prints that she had made

2. Restriction: HNPS Does Not Apply to Indirect Objects

While HNPS can move Direct Objects, it cannot move
· Indirect Objects
· Objects of prepositions

* I sent — a postcard my cousin from London.
* I sent a postcard to — yesterday my cousin from London.

Why?
· Indirect Objects and Prepositional Objects must stay in their fixed positions
· Only heavy Direct Objects can shift rightward.

Extraposition of Subject Clauses

Extraposition is a syntactic movement process where a clausal subject is moved from the beginning of the sentence to the end, with the pronoun "it" inserted in the vacated subject position.

1. Subject Clause in Default Position
In the unmarked word order, the Subject Clause appears at the beginning

Canonical Order
That the film ended so soon was a shame.

- Here, 'That the film ended so soon' functions as the subject of the sentence.

2. Subject Clause After Extraposition
Extraposition moves the Subject Clause to the end of the sentence, and "it" is inserted in the subject position

Extraposed Order
It was a shame that the film ended so soon.

- The dummy subject it is inserted.
- The true Subject Clause that the film ended so soon appears at the end.

3. Why Does Extraposition Happen?
- Improves readability and processing ease

Long Subject Clauses at the beginning can be heavy and difficult to process.
- More natural in spoken English

Extraposition is commonly used in everyday speech.

Extraposition from NP (ENP)

Extraposition from NP (ENP) is a syntactic movement process where a modifying phrase (typically a Prepositional Phrase (PP) or a Relative Clause (RC)) is moved out of a noun phrase (NP) to the end of the sentence.

1. Examples of ENP

① Prepositional Phrase Extraposition from Subject NP
- Canonical Order (No Extraposition)

Six women with yellow hats appeared.
- Extraposed Order

[Six women —] appeared with yellow hats.

What happened?
- The PP with yellow hats was moved from inside the NP Six women to the end of the sentence.
- This confirms that with yellow hats is a constituent of Six women.

② Prepositional Phrase Extraposition from Direct Object NP
- Canonical Order

We employed two people from European Union countries last week.
- Extraposed Order

We employed [two people —] last week from European Union countries.

What happened?
- The PP from European Union countries was moved out of the Direct Object NP two people to the end of the sentence.

③ Relative Clause Extraposition from Subject NP
- Canonical Order

The dogs that were chained to the house escaped.
- Extraposed Order

[The dogs —] escaped that were chained to the house.

What happened?
- The Relative Clause that were chained to the house was moved to the end of the sentence.
- This confirms that the relative clause is a constituent of The dogs.

2. Constraints on ENP

① ENP is more acceptable when:
- The verb phrase (VP) is light (i.e., the verb is intransitive or a raising verb like seem, appear, become).

② ENP is less acceptable when:
- The verb is transitive and has a complex VP.

Example of an awkward ENP sentence
?* [Three men —] noisily left the theatre who were drunk.

This sentence is marked "?" because the relative clause 'who were drunk' does not move naturally in this case.

3. ENP as a Constituency Test

ENP can be used to test whether a string of words forms a single constituent.

Example
- Original Sentence

Six women with yellow hats on their heads appeared.

- If the whole phrase is a single PP constituent, we should be able to extrapose it

[Six women —] appeared with yellow hats on their heads.

- However, if 'with yellow hats' and 'on their heads' are separate PPs, we should be able to extrapose only with yellow hats

* Six women — on their heads appeared with yellow hats.

Extraposition from NP (ENP)

Conclusion
- Since the sentence above is ungrammatical, 'with yellow hats on their heads' must be a single constituent.
- The PP on their heads is actually an adjunct to the Head N hats.

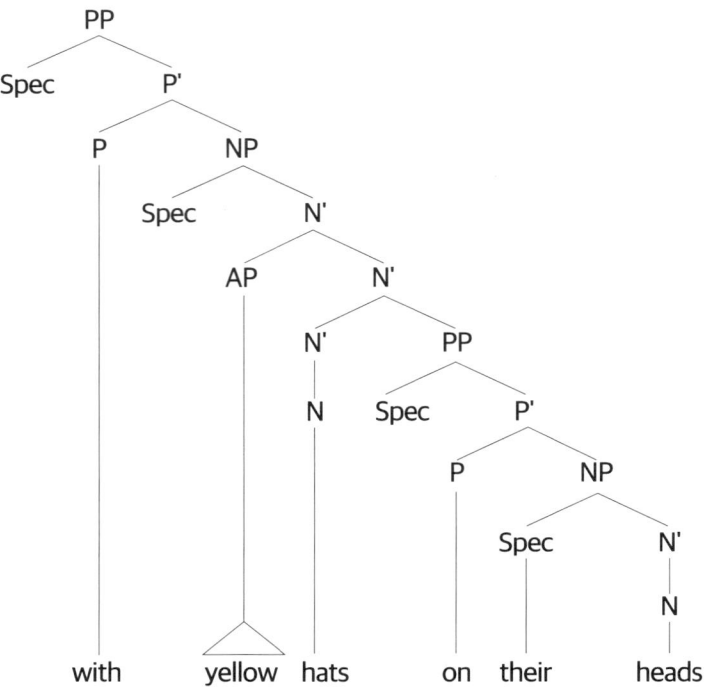

Substitution (Replacement)

One way to check if a group of words is a constituent is by seeing if it can be replaced by something else. This "something else" might be:

- a single word (like a pronoun),
- another group of words,
- or even nothing at all (in the case of ellipsis).

Like movement, substitution is a test that applies to full phrases. However, it can also apply to bar-level constituents (like N' or V'), and even entire clauses.

1. Substitution of Nominal Projections: NP

Consider this sentence
My father admires my mother.

To show that my father and my mother are constituents, we can use the Substitution Test.

- Substitution Test

A sequence of words is a constituent if it can be replaced by a suitable proform.

Here, 'my father' can be replaced by 'he', and 'my mother' by 'her'
He admires her.

This kind of substitution is known as pronominalisation and is common in all natural languages.

For example
Speaker A: What do you think of the guy who wrote that unbelievably boring book on Transformational Grammar?
Speaker B: I can't stand him.

Substitution (Replacement)

Here, 'him' refers back to the entire NP 'the guy who wrote that unbelievably boring book on Transformational Grammar'. Therefore, 'him' is not replacing a noun, but an entire Noun Phrase (NP). So, such pronouns are more accurately called pro-NPs (pro-Noun Phrases).

More generally, since these forms replace constituents, they are known as proforms or pro-constituents. Not all proforms are for NPs. We also have other kinds.

2. Other Phrase Substitution
① pro-PP: Pro-Prepositional Phrase

ⓐ A: Have you ever been to Paris? B: No, I have never been there.
ⓑ Our neighbors will go on holiday on Sunday, and we will leave then too.

Here, there replaces to Paris, and then replaces on Sunday. These are pro-PPs.

② pro-VP: Pro-Verb Phrase
John might [VP go home], and so might Bill.
John might [VP resign his post], as might Sue.

The 'so' and 'as' in second clauses refer back to the VPs in the first clauses. Hence, these are examples of pro-VP substitution.

③ pro-AP: Pro-Adjective Phrase
Many people consider John [AP extremely rude], but I've never found him so.
They say Wayne is [AP very unhappy], and so he is.

Here, 'so' replaces adjective phrases (APs).

3. Substitution of Nominal Projections: N' (One-Substitution)

Besides pronouns replacing full NPs, English also allows substitution of N-bar (N') levels using the word "one".

Mark is a dedicated teacher of language, but Paul is an indifferent one.

Here, one replaces teacher of language, which is not a full NP (because it's preceded by an adjective and a determiner). Thus, one replaces an N'.

- One-Substitution

The proform one replaces N'-constituents.

the [N' book with a red cover] → the one with a red cover

But:
* the one of poems

This is because complements like of poems are sisters to the N, not part of the N'. So, one cannot substitute them.

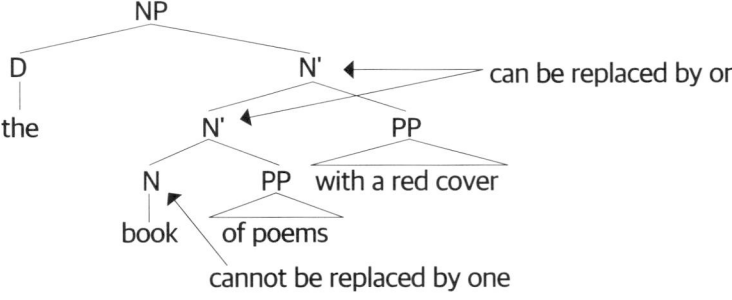

Compare:

This student of chemistry is more industrious than that one.
* The student of physics is taller than the one of chemistry.

Only N' structures (not just N or N + complement) can be replaced by one.

Substitution (Replacement)

4. Substitution of Verbal Projections: VP

We can also substitute VPs using ellipsis (omitting the repeated material).

Bill: Will you please leave the room?
Dawn: OK, I will — !

Here, 'leave the room' is understood but not spoken. This is called VP-Deletion, and it functions as substitution using a null proform (nothing).

Henry: You take a lot of risks.
Jake: I aim to — !

Again, 'take a lot of risks' is omitted and replaced by nothing. Since only constituents can be replaced by proforms, this tells us that take a lot of risks is a VP.

5. Substitution of Verbal Projections: V' (Do So-Substitution)

Now let's look at V' substitution using the proform "do so".

ⓐ Dawn cleaned the windows diligently.
ⓑ Dawn cleaned the windows diligently, and Sean did so too.
ⓒ Dawn cleaned the windows diligently, but Sean did so lazily.

In ⓐ, 'did so' replaces the entire VP cleaned the windows diligently.
In ⓑ, it replaces cleaned the windows and leaves behind the adjunct lazily.

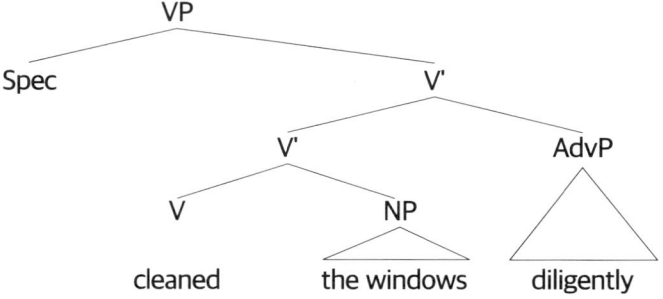

- Do So Substitution

The expression 'do so' replaces V'-constituents.

Other examples

Barry hired a big Jaguar, and Milly did so too.
Lenny sent Will a postcard, and Gemma did so too.

But:

* Barry hired a big Jaguar, and Milly did so a Volkswagen.
* Lenny sent Will a postcard, and Gemma did so a present.

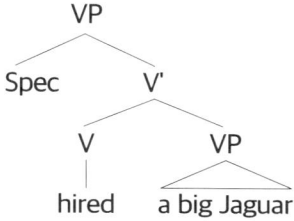

These are ungrammatical because 'do so' cannot replace only part of the V'—it must replace V + its complements as a whole.

6. V'-Deletion

V'-deletion also targets verbal bar-level constituents.

Consider

Dawn cleaned the windows diligently.
Dawn will clean the windows diligently, but Sean will — lazily.

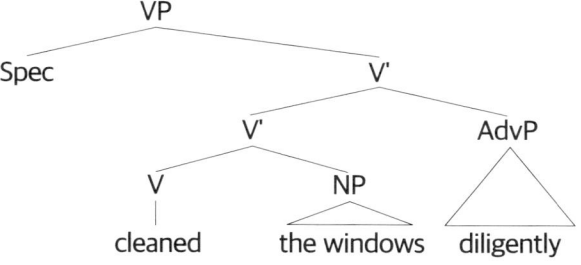

Here, 'clean the windows' is deleted, and what's left (lazily) is an adjunct. So again, 'clean the windows' must be a V', and this is another example of V'-Deletion using a null proform.

The Coordination Test

Coordination refers to linking two or more strings using coordinating conjunctions like and, or, and but. This process can help us test whether a string of words is a constituent.

- Coordination Test

Only constituents can be coordinated.

This means that if two strings can be joined using a coordinating conjunction and the resulting sentence is grammatical, then each of those strings must be a constituent.

1. Ordinary Coordination

Let's begin with a simple sentence

Frank washed his shirts yesterday.

In this sentence, we can propose a basic structure where different parts of the sentence (subject, verb, object, adverbial) form constituents. The coordination test allows us to check the constituent status of those parts by trying to coordinate them with similar elements.

Examples
- Frank washed and ironed his shirts yesterday.

(Coordination of main verbs)

- Frank washed his shirts and polished his shoes yesterday.

(Coordination of lower V'-level phrases)

- Frank washed his shirts yesterday and last week.

(Coordination of temporal adjuncts)

- Frank washed his shirts yesterday and polished his shoes last week.

(Coordination of higher V'-level phrases)

All of these are grammatical, so each coordinated part must be a constituent.

- Same Category Constraint

Generally, only constituents of the same syntactic category can be coordinated.

Consider

John wrote to Mary and to Fred. (PP and PP)
John wrote a letter and a postcard. (NP and NP)
* John wrote a letter and to Fred. (NP and PP)
* John wrote to Fred and a letter. (PP and NP)

Thus,
- Only identical categories can be conjoined.

But there are exceptions in predicative environments—such as after verbs like be—where different phrase types can be coordinated

John is a banker and extremely rich. (NP and AP)
John is moody and under the weather. (AP and PP)
John is a superb athlete and in a class of his own. (NP and PP)

These are accepted because predicative coordination is more flexible.

The Coordination Test

2. Shared Constituent Coordination: Right Node Raising

Another useful test is called Right Node Raising (RNR). This occurs when two clauses share a constituent that appears only once—at the end of the sentence.

John walked —, and Mary ran —, up the hill.
John denied —, but Fred admitted —, complicity in the crime.
John will —, and Mary may —, go to the party.

Each sentence is grammatical. The shared phrase (e.g., up the hill) is part of both clauses and thus is a constituent of each.

By contrast,
* John rang —, and Harry picked up Mary's sister.

This is ungrammatical because rang up and picked up are phrasal verbs, and the position of up differs structurally. In the first conjunct, 'up' is part of rang up, and in the second, it's part of picked up. They cannot share the same constituent.

So,
- Shared constituent coordination is only possible when the shared string is a constituent in each conjunct.

This kind of coordination is called Right Node Raising because the shared constituent appears at the rightmost edge (or "right node") of the sentence.

3. Coordination of Complementizer Phrases (CPs)

Now let's consider coordination at the CP (Complementizer Phrase) level. In basic phrase structure theory, TP and CP rules don't seem to follow the X-bar format, but they can be revised to fit it.

- CP → (C) TP
- TP → DP (T) VP

We can reanalyze (1a) in X-bar terms:

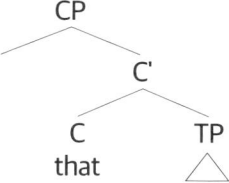

This structure treats that as the head of CP, taking TP as its complement, and leaving an empty specifier.

But do all clauses have CPs?
It may seem that only embedded clauses require CPs because they include an overt complementizer like that:

John thinks that the asparagus is yummy.
* That the asparagus is yummy.

However, evidence suggests that even root clauses (main clauses) may contain a null complementizer.

For instance,
Asparagus grows in California.

→ This may actually be:
[CP [C' Ø [TP Asparagus grows in California]]]

Further support comes from coordination. Only CPs can be coordinated with CPs.

The Coordination Test

Consider:
[You can lead a horse to water] but [will it drink]?

In the second clause (will it drink), subject-auxiliary inversion indicates that there's a Ø[+Q] null complementizer. For this coordination to be possible, the first clause must also be a CP—with a Ø[-Q] complementizer.

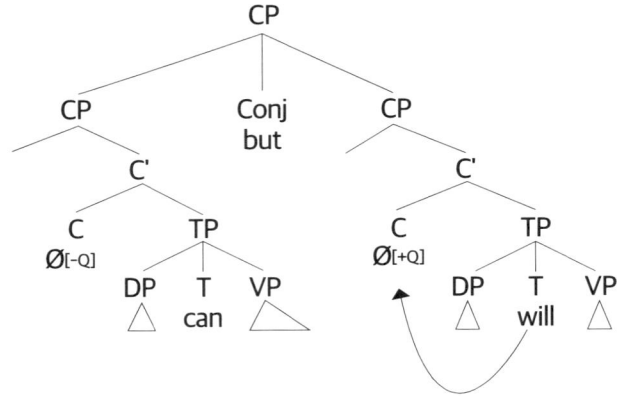

Thus,

- Even statements (root clauses) must have a null CP layer.

From this point forward, we assume that every clause, even simple main clauses, has an underlying CP structure, although we may omit it in diagrams for simplicity.

Complementizers

In English syntax, complementizers are words that introduce complement clauses—these are clauses that function as the object or subject of a verb.

Examples of complementizers include: that, for, whether, and if.

Complementizers can be classified based on two criteria:

1. Syntactic Function: Interrogative or Noninterrogative

- Interrogative complementizers are used with questions (indirect questions).

Example: I don't know whether he will come.

- Noninterrogative complementizers are used with statements.

Example: I think that he will come.

2. Morphological Form: Finite or Nonfinite

- Finite complementizers introduce clauses with a finite verb (a verb marked for tense).

Example: that in I hope that he arrives on time.

- Nonfinite complementizers introduce clauses with nonfinite verbs (e.g., infinitives).

Example: for in I hope for him to arrive on time.

Examples of Each Complementizer:

① That = Noninterrogative + Finite

I'm anxious [that you should arrive on time]

* I'm anxious [that you to arrive on time]

→ "that" does not introduce infinitive (nonfinite) clauses.

② For = Noninterrogative + Nonfinite

I'm anxious [for you to arrive on time]

* I'm anxious [for you should arrive on time]

→ "for" does not introduce finite clauses.

③ Whether and If = Interrogative
I don't know [whether I should agree]
I don't know [if I should agree]
I don't know [whether to agree]
* I don't know [if to agree]

→ "whether" works with both finite and nonfinite clauses.
→ "if" only works with finite clauses.

3. Feature Representation of Complementizers
We can use two binary features:
- [±WH] → whether the complementizer introduces an interrogative clause
- [±FINITE] → whether the complementizer introduces a finite clause

Complementizer	[±WH]	[±FINITE]
that	[-WH]	[+FINITE]
for	[-WH]	[-FINITE]
whether	[+WH]	[±FINITE]
if	[+WH]	[+FINITE]

4. Complementizer Phrase (CP) Structure Rule
We can represent the complementizer slot in a sentence with a rule:

C → [±WH, ±FINITE]

This allows the CP (Complementizer Phrase) to have any of the following combinations:

- [+WH, +FINITE] → filled by whether or if
- [+WH, -FINITE] → filled only by whether
- [-WH, +FINITE] → filled by that
- [-WH, -FINITE] → filled by for

The Cleft and Pseudocleft Test

Cleft and pseudocleft constructions are special sentence forms in English that allow speakers to highlight or emphasize a particular part of a sentence. These constructions are useful not only for discourse purposes but also for testing constituency.

1. Basic Structure

Both constructions involve restructuring a sentence so that a specific phrase—called the focus—is placed in a prominent syntactic position.

Here are the skeletal forms:
- Cleft Sentence

It + form of BE + FOCUS + who/that ...

e.g. It was Frank who washed his shirts yesterday.

- Pseudocleft Sentence

Wh-word + clause + form of BE + FOCUS

e.g. What Frank did was wash his shirts yesterday.

In a cleft sentence, the focus appears immediately after the verb "be", while in a pseudocleft, the focus comes at the end of the sentence. In both cases, this special structure brings attention to a single constituent.

2. Examples

- Clefts

It was your big brother who built this house.
It is her artificial smile that I can't stand.
It was for Mary that John bought the flowers (not for Susan).
It was just last week that Mary offered me the job.

- Pseudoclefts

What I can't stand is her artificial smile.
What John said to Mary was that he intended to run for parliament.
What I like for breakfast is fried noodles.

These sentences show that the cleft or pseudocleft structure places emphasis on a single constituent that conveys new or important information.

The Cleft and Pseudocleft Test

3. The Test

The Cleft and Pseudocleft Test works by checking whether a string of words can appear in the focus position of these constructions. If it can, then it is a constituent.

Cleft and Pseudocleft Test
- Only constituents can occur in the focus position of a cleft or pseudocleft sentence.

Let's look at some ungrammatical examples to see what happens when the focused element is not a proper constituent.

- Clefts
* It was [a book] [to Mary] that John gave.
* It was [your big] who built this house brother.

Here, either multiple constituents are placed in focus (which is not allowed), or the string is not a complete syntactic unit.

- Pseudoclefts
* What John gave was [a book] [to Mary].
* What I can't stand smile is [her artificial].

Again, these examples are ungrammatical or marginal because the focus position is occupied by non-constituents or multiple separate constituents.

The Insertion Test

The Insertion Test is another useful tool for identifying constituents. This test is based on the syntactic behavior of adverbials, especially their possible positions in a sentence.

Certain adverbs in English can only be inserted into specific positions in the sentence. The positions where an adverb can or cannot appear depend on what kind of constituent it is modifying.

By observing where an adverb can be inserted, we can infer the boundaries of constituents—for example, whether something is a VP or S.

1. Two Types of Adverbs

From a syntactic perspective, English has two major types of adverbs

① S-Adverbs (sentence-level adverbs)
→ certainly, probably, fortunately
→ These modify the entire sentence and attach to the S-node.

② VP-Adverbs (verb phrase-level adverbs)
→ completely, entirely, thoroughly
→ These modify the verb phrase and attach to the VP-node.

Let's look at the differences in their distribution using the following sentence:

The team can rely on my support.

We'll try inserting certainly and completely into various positions in this sentence to see what is allowed.

The Insertion Test

2. Examples of Insertion

① Certainly / *completely, the team can rely on my support.

② The *certainly / *completely team can rely on my support.

③ The team certainly / *completely can rely on my support.

④ The team can certainly / completely rely on my support.

⑤ The team can rely completely / *certainly on my support.

⑥ The team can rely on *certainly / *completely my support.

⑦ The team can rely on my *certainly / *completely support.

⑧ The team can rely on my support completely / certainly.

3. Syntactic Explanation

Based on these patterns, we can make the following generalizations:

- S-adverbs like certainly can only be attached to an S-node.
- VP-adverbs like completely can only be attached to a VP-node.

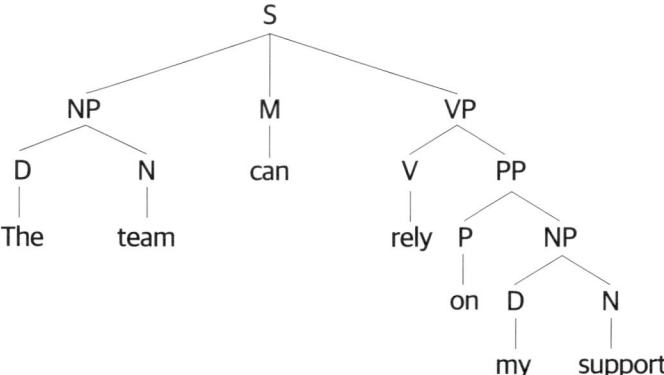

Stand-alone Test (The Constituent Response Test or The Sentence Fragment Test)

Another way to determine whether a group of words forms a constituent is to use the Sentence Fragment Test. This test is based on how we typically answer open interrogatives (questions using what, who, where, etc.).

1. Basic Principle
When someone asks an open-ended question, we often respond with a short phrase instead of a full sentence.

The important point is this:
- Only constituents can serve as responses to open interrogatives.

This is known as the Stand-alone Test(Constituent Response Test or The Sentence Fragment Test)

2. Examples
①
A: What did you buy at the flea market?
B-①: An old Swedish wineskin.
B-②: * An old Swedish.

In the grammatical answer, an old Swedish wineskin is a full noun phrase (NP) and a constituent. In the ungrammatical version, an old Swedish is not a complete constituent—it lacks a noun head—and sounds incomplete.

②
Dick: Where did you buy this bread?
Frances: In the supermarket.

Here, in the supermarket is a prepositional phrase (PP) and a valid constituent, so the response is grammatical.

Prepositional Verbs and Phrasal Verbs

1. Structural Differences

Although they may look similar, prepositional verbs and phrasal verbs have different internal structures. Let's compare:

ⓐ Drunks would get off the bus.
ⓑ Drunks would put off the customers.

At first glance, both seem to follow the same pattern: [Verb + off + NP].
But structurally, they are different.

- In ⓐ, the preposition off combines with the following noun phrase [the bus] to form a Prepositional Phrase (PP): [off the bus]. The verb get is therefore classified as a Prepositional Verb, because it takes a Prepositional Phrase as its complement.
- In ⓑ, the word off does not go with the noun phrase [the customers], but rather combines with the verb put to form a Phrasal Verb: put off. This means put off acts like a single, compound verb.

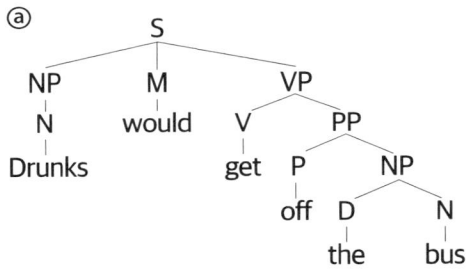

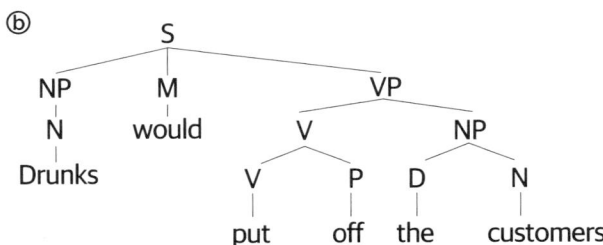

2. Movement Test

Only full phrases can be moved to the front of a sentence.

ⓐ [Off the bus] would get an old lady.

ⓑ * [Off the customers] they certainly would put.

This tells us that "off the bus" is a PP, while "off the customers" is not a phrase.

3. Sentence-Fragment Test

Only full phrases can be used as sentence fragments.

ⓐ

A: Did he get off the train?

B: No, off the bus.

ⓑ

A: Would drunks put off the waitresses?

* B: No, off the customers.

Again, only prepositional verbs allow this, not phrasal verbs.

4. Adverb Placement

VP adverbs (like quickly, completely) can appear inside VPs.

ⓐ Drunks would get slowly off the bus.

ⓑ * Drunks would put completely off the customers.

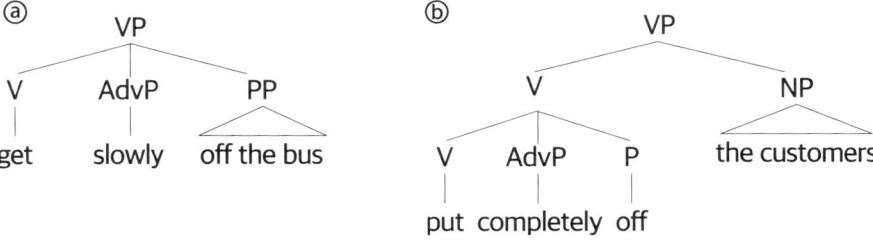

The adverb cannot interrupt a phrasal verb, which shows that put off behaves like a unit.

Prepositional Verbs and Phrasal Verbs

5. Coordination

Phrases of the same type can be coordinated.

ⓐ Drunks would get [off the bus] and [on the train].

ⓑ * Drunks would put off the customers and off the waitresses.

Only real phrases (like PPs) can be coordinated properly.

6. Ellipsis (Gapping)

ⓐ Drunks would get off the bus, and junkies ~~would get~~ off the train.

ⓑ * Drunks would put off the customers, and junkies ~~would put~~ off the waitresses.

Better: Drunks would put off the customers, and junkies ~~would put off~~ the waitresses.

In phrasal verbs, the verb and particle behave as a unit and must be kept together.

7. Pronominalization

We know that noun phrases (NPs) can be coordinated with other NPs. For example:

ⓐ Drunks would get off [the bus] and [the train]

ⓑ Drunks would put off [the customers] and [the waitresses]

Since both [the bus] and [the customers] behave like NPs, we expect that they should be replaceable by pronouns like it or them.

This expectation holds for prepositional verbs like get off:

ⓐ The trouble with the bus was that drunks would want to get off it every few miles.

However, it does not hold for phrasal verbs like put off:

ⓑ * What worries me about the customers is whether drunks would put off them.

This suggests an important difference:
- Prepositional verbs (like get off) can take pronouns as their object.
- Phrasal verbs (like put off) cannot take pronouns in the same way—unless the pronoun appears in a different position.

In fact, this is a bit more complicated. Consider:

ⓐ * Drunks would put off them.
ⓑ Drunks would put them off.

As you can see, phrasal verbs can take pronominal objects, but only if the pronoun comes between the verb and the particle (here, off).

And this pattern holds even for regular noun phrases:
ⓐ Drunks would put [the customers] off.

By contrast, prepositional verbs do not allow the preposition to be separated from its object:
ⓑ * Drunks would get the bus off.

Finally, when the entire VP (Verb Phrase) is fronted for emphasis, the particle stays with the object—showing that it is a single unit:

The manager said that drunks would put the customers off, and [put the customers off] they certainly would.

This confirms that in sentences like 'Drunks would put the customers off.', the verb and particle form a single Phrasal Verb, and the object fits inside the verb phrase structure.

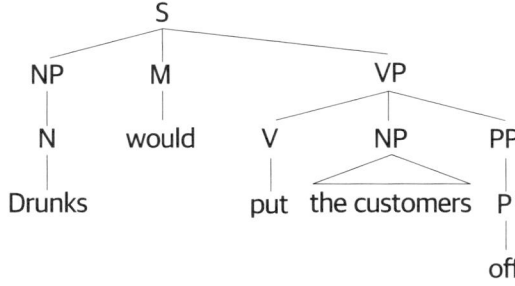

Verb Complements

Intro

The concept of argumenthood is closely connected to constituency. To understand how verbs interact with other elements in a sentence, we must examine the predicate-argument structure.

A predicate is a linguistic expression—often a verb or verb phrase—that requires one or more arguments to form a complete sentence. The arguments are the constituents that the predicate needs in order to be semantically and syntactically complete.

Consider the following examples:
- <u>Penny</u> **admires** <u>Judith.</u>
- <u>Imelda</u> **sent** <u>Darren presents.</u>
- <u>Pam</u> **thinks** <u>that she is clever.</u>
- <u>Being here</u> **annoys** <u>me.</u>

In each sentence:
- The predicate is shown in bold.
- The arguments (the required participants in the event or state described by the predicate) are underlined.

Intro

1. Number of Arguments

In English, a predicate typically requires:

- At least one argument
- Usually no more than three arguments.

2. Identifying Arguments vs. Adjuncts

Sometimes, it is easy to tell whether a word or phrase is an argument of a verb. In other cases, it's more complex. For these tricky cases, linguists use a set of diagnostic tests to determine whether a particular element is an argument (necessary) or an adjunct (optional).

Some of the tests for argumenthood include:

- Meaning test: Does the element contribute core meaning to the predicate?
- Dummy element substitution: Can it be replaced with a dummy (like it)?
- Idiom chunk test: Is it part of an idiomatic expression?
- Passivization test: Can it become the subject in a passive construction?

These tests help us determine whether a constituent is required by the verb (i.e., an argument) or is merely adding extra information (i.e., an adjunct).

The Believe-Type Construction

1. Meaning

The number and type of arguments a verb takes are largely determined by its meaning. In the case of the verb believe, we start with basic examples:

ⓐ Ed believes the story.
→ believe is a two-place predicate, taking:

- a Subject (Ed) - the believer
- a Direct Object (the story) - what is believed

ⓑ Ed believes that the story is false.
→ Here, the object is not a noun phrase but a clause (that the story is false). This shows that believe can also take clausal complements, not just NPs.

Both the story in ⓐ and that the story is false in ⓑ are Direct Objects, bearing thematic roles such as:

- Patient (in ⓐ): the story is what is believed
- Proposition (in ⓑ): the entire clause represents the content of the belief

ⓒ Ed believes the story to be false.

At first glance, this structure seems to contain two arguments after believe:

- the story (possibly a Direct Object)
- to be false (a non-finite clause)

This leads to the question: is the story in ⓒ really a Direct Object of believe?

The Believe-Type Construction

- **Argument 1: Passive Evidence**

ⓓ The story is believed ___ to be false by Ed.

The fact that the story can be fronted in a passive sentence suggests it functions like a Direct Object. Moreover:

ⓔ Ed believes him to be a traitor.
→ him appears in accusative case, as expected for an object.

ⓕ Ed believes that he is a traitor.
→ he appears in nominative case, as the subject of the embedded clause.

These case differences seem to support an analysis where him/the story is directly selected by believe as a Direct Object.

- **Argument 2: Thematic Mismatch**

However, there is a semantic problem: if the story is a Direct Object of believe in ⓒ, the meaning should match ⓐ (Ed believes the story).

But in ⓒ, the sentence means that:

Ed believes [that the story is false].

So semantically, the story is not something that is believed; instead, it is the subject of the clause 'the story to be false.' This suggests that the whole string 'the story to be false' functions as a clausal complement (i.e., a single constituent) selected by believe.

- **Conclusion:** In ⓒ, the story is not a Direct Object of believe, but rather the subject of the embedded infinitival clause. The clause 'the story to be false' is a single clausal argument of believe.

2. Dummy Elements and Idiom Chunks

English includes certain dummy elements—words with no referential meaning.

These include:

- Nonreferential it:

It is raining.
It is cold.

- Existential there:

There are a number of solutions to this problem.
There has been an increase in crime in America.

Because these elements carry no thematic role, they cannot function as arguments like true Subjects or Direct Objects. Therefore, if such an element appears after believe, it cannot be the Direct Object—it must instead be the Subject of an embedded clause because nonreferential it and existential there (also called expletive or pleonastic elements) always occur in the Subject position.

Ed believes it always to be raining in London.
Ed believes there to be a traitor in the company.

In both cases, it and there are subjects of the non-finite clause (it always to be raining, there to be a traitor), not Direct Objects of believe.

The same reasoning applies to idiom chunks—phrases whose meaning breaks down if their parts are replaced:

The coast is clear.
The fat is in the fire.

Ed believes [the coast to be clear].
Ed believes [the fat to be in the fire].

The Believe-Type Construction

These idioms rely on fixed phrases. The constituents the coast and the fat cannot be changed or omitted. They function as Subjects of the embedded clauses, not as arguments of believe.

- Conclusion: If dummy elements or idiom chunks appear in believe + NP + to-infinitive structures, the NP must be the subject of the infinitival clause, not a Direct Object of believe.

3. Passivization

Another useful diagnostic is passivization.

ⓐ Ed believes [the jury to have given the wrong verdict].
ⓑ Ed believes [the wrong verdict to have been given by the jury].

These two sentences differ in the surface structure but not in meaning. The ability to passivize the clause without changing meaning supports the analysis that:

- the jury and the wrong verdict are not Direct Objects of believe
- Instead, they are constituents inside the embedded clause

Compare:
ⓒ The jury is believed [to have given the wrong verdict] by Ed.

Here, the main clause is passivized (The jury is believed), showing a different operation from what happens in ⓑ, where the subordinate clause is passivized.

- Generalization:

If the NP following a verb in a verb + NP + to-infinitive structure can undergo passivization within the embedded clause, then that NP is likely the subject of the embedded clause, not the Direct Object of the main verb.

The Persuade-Type Construction

1. Meaning

Let's examine the following example:

ⓐ Ed persuaded Brian to interview Melanie.

Here, the meaning of persuade clearly establishes a direct relationship between:

- Ed (the persuader, Subject)
- Brian (the persuadee, Direct Object)
- to interview Melanie (the resulting action)

This is unlike believe, where the postverbal NP (Brian, in a sentence like Ed believes Brian to interview Melanie) would not be the Direct Object.

In ⓐ, Brian is affected by the act of persuasion, meaning he plays the experiencer/patient role with respect to persuade. Thus, Brian functions as a Direct Object (DO).

- Conclusion: In the persuade + NP + to-infinitive construction, the NP (Brian) is the Direct Object of the main verb.

The Persuade-Type Construction

2. Dummy Elements and Idiom Chunks

To further confirm that the postverbal NP is a Direct Object, we can apply tests involving dummy elements and idioms.

Recall:
- Dummy elements like it and there can only appear in Subject positions and cannot bear thematic roles.
- Idiom chunks rely on fixed forms and do not normally function as arguments outside their idiomatic structure.

Let's try placing dummy elements in the NP position after persuade:

* Ed persuaded it to be hot in the room.
* Ed persuaded there to be a party.

These are ungrammatical because it and there cannot function as Direct Objects—they do not receive a thematic role from persuade.

Now try using idiom chunks:

* Ed persuaded the coast to be clear.
* Ed persuaded the fat to be in the fire.

Again, these are unacceptable. The NP after persuade must be a referential, animate argument that can participate in the act of persuasion—conditions not satisfied by either dummy elements or idioms.

- Conclusion: The NP in this construction cannot be a dummy or idiom chunk, supporting its status as a Direct Object that receives a thematic role from persuade.

3. Passivization

Let's now test this structure using passivization.

ⓐ Ed persuaded Brian to interview Melanie.
ⓑ Ed persuaded Melanie to be interviewed by Brian.

Both sentences involve a clear persuasion event directed at a person (Brian in ⓐ, Melanie in ⓑ). Even though the embedded clause has been passivized in ⓑ, there is still a thematic relationship between Ed and Melanie. This tells us that the NP after persuade—whether Brian or Melanie—is a Direct Object of the main verb.

Contrast this with the believe construction, where passivization showed that the NP was not a Direct Object but rather the subject of the embedded clause.

Additionally, the sentence in ⓒ illustrates coreference between the Direct Object of the main clause and the subject of the embedded clause, marked with co-indexation:

ⓒ Ed persuaded Brian$_i$ [Ø$_i$ to interview Melanie].

Here, the null subject (PRO) of the embedded clause is understood to refer to Brian, confirming the syntactic and semantic link between the two positions.

- Conclusion: Passivization confirms that the NP following persuade is a Direct Object that plays a key role in the meaning of the sentence.

The Want-Type Construction

1. Meaning

Consider the sentence:

Kate wants Ralph to get out of her life.

What exactly does Kate want? Not Ralph himself, but rather a situation in which Ralph gets out of her life. Situations are described by propositions, so the true object of want in this case is the entire infinitival clause: Ralph to get out of her life.

This suggests the following structure:
- Kate = subject and experiencer of desire
- Ralph to get out of her life = clausal complement (a nonfinite clause functioning as Direct Object)
- Ralph = subject of the embedded infinitival clause

- Conclusion: In the want + NP + to-infinitive construction, the NP (Ralph) is not the Direct Object of want, but the subject of the embedded clause.

2. Dummy Elements and Idiom Chunks

This conclusion is further supported by tests involving dummy elements and idiom chunks.

Let's look at dummy elements first:

ⓐ Kate wanted it to rain on Ralph's birthday.
ⓑ Ralph wanted there to be a ceasefire between him and Kate.

In both sentences:

- it (nonreferential dummy subject)
- there (existential dummy subject)

appear in subject positions of the embedded clause, not as Direct Objects of want. These elements are semantically empty, and since arguments must have thematic roles, they cannot function as Direct Objects of want. Therefore, the entire clause (it to rain, there to be a ceasefire) must be the actual complement.

Next, consider idiom chunks:

ⓒ Kate wants the coast to be clear.
ⓓ Kate doesn't want the fat to be in the fire.

These idioms only make sense if the coast and the fat are part of the embedded clause. They cannot be Direct Objects of want, since their meanings are tied to the full idiomatic expressions.

- Conclusion: Dummy elements and idiom chunks can only function as subjects of embedded clauses, reinforcing that want selects a clausal complement, not the NP alone.

The Want-Type Construction

3. Passivization

Passivization provides more insight into the syntactic behavior of want.

Consider:
ⓐ Kate wanted Janet to poison Ralph.
ⓑ Kate wanted Ralph to be poisoned by Janet.

In both cases, the propositional meaning remains the same: Kate desires a specific outcome. The NP after want (Janet in ⓐ, Ralph in ⓑ) does not receive a direct thematic role from want; rather, they are participants within the embedded clause.

This behavior aligns want with the believe-type structure.

But there is a crucial difference: believe allows passivization of the main clause, whereas want does not.

ⓒ Ed believes the jury to have given the wrong verdict.
ⓓ The jury is believed to have given the wrong verdict by Ed.
ⓔ Kate wanted Janet to poison Ralph.
ⓕ * Janet was wanted to poison Ralph by Kate.

The passive in ⓕ is ungrammatical, revealing that want does not permit main clause passivization in the same way believe does.

This difference also appears when believe and want take simple noun phrase Direct Objects:

(47) Ed believed the wild allegations.
(48) The wild allegations were believed by Ed.
(49) Ed wanted a new CD player.
(50) ? * A new CD player was wanted by Ed. (awkward or marginal at best)

- Conclusion: While want and believe both take clausal complements, only believe allows passivization of the main clause. This indicates that want behaves differently in terms of syntax, even when the clause it selects looks structurally similar.

Summary: Verb + NP + to-infinitive Constructions

We have examined three distinct types of verb + NP + to-infinitive constructions, focusing on the verbs believe, persuade, and want. While they share similar surface structures, they differ significantly in argument structure, thematic relations, and syntactic behavior.

Consider the following examples:

ⓐ Ed believes the story to be false.
ⓑ Ed persuaded Brian to interview Melanie.
ⓒ Kate wants Ralph to get out of her life.

Each example contains:

- a main clause subject (Ed, Kate)
- a postverbal NP (the story, Brian, Ralph)
- a to-infinitival clause

However, the syntactic and semantic status of the postverbal NP differs across constructions.

Verb Classes and Their Properties

Verb Class	Structure	NP Role	Class
Believe-type	V + [NP + to-infinitive]	subject of embedded clause	believe, consider, expect, intend, know, suppose, understand
Persuade-type	V + [NP] + [to-infinitive]	DO of main verb & subject of clause	advise, convince, notify
Want-type	V + [NP + to-infinitive]	subject of embedded clause	want, demand, hate, hope, love, prefer, wish

※ These lists are not exhaustive, and some verbs may occur in multiple patterns depending on context.

Raising and Control

Raising and Control Predicates

Some verbs in English select a to-infinitival VP as their complement. On the surface, sentences with these verbs may look similar—but a closer syntactic and semantic analysis reveals two distinct types of constructions: control constructions and raising constructions.

1. Surface Similarity
Consider the following examples:

ⓐ John tries to fix the computer.
ⓑ John seems to fix the computer.

Both sentences contain:
- a subject (John),
- a main verb (tries / seems), and
- a to-infinitival complement (to fix the computer).

Now compare:

ⓒ Mary persuaded John to fix the computer.
ⓓ Mary expected John to fix the computer.

In both ⓒ and ⓓ, the verb takes:

- an NP (John), and
- a to-infinitival VP (to fix the computer).

Although these sentence types are structurally similar on the surface, they differ in how the subject of the embedded clause relates to the rest of the sentence. This difference is what motivates the distinction between control and raising predicates.

2. Control vs. Raising Predicates
We divide the verbs (and some adjectives) into two major classes:

Control Verbs/Adjectives	Raising Verbs/Adjectives
try, persuade, eager, hope, promise, consider, etc.	seem, expect, certain, appear, happen, believe, likely, etc.

Raising and Control Predicates

① Control Verbs

Control verbs are also called equi-verbs. In a control construction, the subject (or object) of the main verb controls the unexpressed subject of the infinitival clause.

ⓐ John tries to fix the computer.

Here, it is John who is doing the fixing. The understood subject of the embedded VP (to fix the computer) is co-referential with the matrix subject John.

This relationship is shown in the deep structure:

ⓑ John tries [(for) John to fix the computer].

The second instance of John in ⓑ is deleted at the surface level, but it remains present in interpretation. This is why such verbs are called control verbs—the subject controls the embedded subject.

② Raising Verbs

Raising verbs, in contrast, do not assign any thematic role to their subject. Instead, the subject originates inside the infinitival clause and is raised to the subject position of the main clause.

ⓐ John seems to fix the computer.

John is not the subject because of the main verb seem—seem does not semantically select John. Instead, John originates in the embedded clause (to fix the computer) and is raised into the matrix subject position.

This is shown in the deep structure:
△ seems [John to fix the computer].

To derive the surface structure, John is moved up in of the matrix clause. This process is called raising, an because it triggers this kind of movement.

Differences Between Raising and Control Verbs

Although raising and control constructions can appear similar on the surface, they differ in key syntactic and semantic properties. This section outlines five major areas of distinction.

1. Subject Raising and Control

① Semantic Role of the Subject

One major difference is whether the main verb assigns a semantic role to its subject.

John tries to be honest.
John seems to be honest.

Paraphrased:
John makes efforts for himself to be honest. (→ John = agent of try)
It seems that John is honest. (→ John = no agent role from seem)

- Control Verbs like try assign a semantic role (e.g., agent) to their subject.
- Raising Verbs like seem do not assign a semantic role to the subject.

② Expletive Subjects

Since raising verbs don't assign a semantic role to their subject, expletives (it, there) can appear in the subject position:

It tends to be warm in September.
It seems to bother Kim that they resigned.

But with control verbs, expletives are ungrammatical:
* It(There) tries to be warm in September.
* It(There) hopes to bother Kim that they resigned.

The same applies to adjectives:
It is easy to please John. (raising)
* It is eager to please Maja. (control)

Differences Between Raising and Control Verbs

③ Subcategorization and Subject Selection

In raising constructions, the embedded predicate determines the properties of the subject:

Stephen seemed [to be intelligent.] (intelligent requires animate subject)
It seems [to be easy to fool Ben.] (expletive it is fine)
There is likely [to be a letter in the mailbox.]
Tabs are likely [to be kept on participants.]

Unacceptable combinations occur when the subject doesn't match the embedded predicate's requirements:

* There seemed [to be intelligent.]
* John seems [to be easy to fool Ben.]
* John is likely [to be a letter in the mailbox.]
* John is likely [to be kept on participants.]

By contrast, control predicates determine the subject's properties themselves:

Sandy tried [to eat oysters.]
* There tried [to be riots in Seoul.]
* It tried [to bother me that Chris lied.]
* Tabs try [to be kept on Bob.]
* That he is clever is eager [to be obvious.]

④ Selectional Restrictions

Verbs often impose semantic selectional restrictions on their subjects or objects

The king thanked the man.
The king thanked the throne. (inanimate object)
? The king thanked the deer. (marginal)
The castle thanked the deer. (non-sentient subject)

The color red is his favorite color.
The color red understands the issues.

The color red seems to be his favorite color. (raising verb seems allows non-sentient subject)
The color red tried to be his favorite color. (control verb tried requires sentient subject)

Key Point
- In raising, the subject is semantically selected by the embedded verb, not the matrix verb.
- In control, the subject is selected by the main verb.

⑤ Meaning Preservation and Idioms
Because raising verbs assign no semantic role to their subjects, idiomatic meanings can be preserved.

The cat seems to be out of the bag. (idiom retained)
* The cat tries to be out of the bag. (idiom lost)

The dentist is likely to examine Pat.
Pat is likely to be examined by the dentist.
(→ semantically equivalent with likely, a raising predicate)

The dentist is eager to examine Pat.
Pat is eager to be examined by the dentist.
(→ different meanings due to eager, a control predicate)

Differences Between Raising and Control Verbs

2. Object Raising and Control
Similar contrasts appear in object raising vs. object control constructions.

Compare:

Stephen believed Ben to be careful. (raising)
Stephen persuaded Ben to be careful. (control)

• Only the raising verb believe allows expletive objects:

Stephen believed it to be easy to please Maja.
* Stephen persuaded it to be easy to please Maja.

Stephen believed there to be a fountain in the park.
* Stephen persuaded there to be a fountain in the park.

• Idioms behave the same:
Stephen believed the cat to be out of the bag. (idiom preserved)
* Stephen persuaded the cat to be out of the bag. (idiom lost)

• Passivization also distinguishes the two:
The dentist was believed to have examined Pat.
Pat was believed to have been examined by the dentist.
→ (believe: no change in meaning)

The dentist was persuaded to examine Pat.
Pat was persuaded to be examined by the dentist.
→ (persuade: clear change in who is persuaded)

Tough Movement & Subject Raising

1. Tough Movement Sentences

Tough movement refers to a syntactic process where the object of an infinitival clause is moved into the subject position of the main clause.

Consider the following:

ⓐ It is easy [to understand this lesson].
ⓑ This lesson is easy [to understand ___].

• In ⓐ, the clause "to understand this lesson" is an extraposed infinitive clause.
• In ⓑ, the object "this lesson" has been moved into the main clause subject position. This process is called tough movement.

Tough movement can also apply when the infinitive clause includes a subject:

ⓐ It is easy for John to understand this lesson.
ⓑ This lesson is easy for John to understand.

Tough movement can also involve the object of a preposition within the infinitival clause:

ⓐ It's a real pleasure to work with John.
ⓑ John is a real pleasure to work with.

Tough movement is only possible when the main verb is be (or something similar), followed by:
• an ease/difficulty adjective (e.g., easy, hard, difficult, tough, pleasant, impossible, dangerous, fun, simple, wonderful)
• an ease/difficulty NP (e.g., a pleasure, a chore, a cinch, a snap, a pain, a piece of cake).

If these conditions are not met, the sentence becomes ungrammatical:

ⓐ It is possible to see the director.
ⓑ * The director is possible to see.
ⓒ It is a real honor to work with Professor Hobson.
ⓓ * Professor Hobson is a real honor to work with.

Tough Movement & Subject Raising

2. Subject Raising Sentences

Some verbs such as seem, appear, and happen can also appear with infinitive clauses, where the subject of the infinitive clause is raised into the main clause subject position:

ⓐ It seems [that Edith enjoys my company].
ⓑ Edith seems [to enjoy my company].

In sentence ⓑ, Edith has been moved from the embedded subject position to the main clause subject position. This process is called Subject Raising.

We can represent this movement as:

ⓐ It seems [Edith to enjoy my company].
ⓑ <u>Edith</u> seems [_____ to enjoy my company].

Subject raising also occurs with adjectives expressing probability, such as likely, unlikely, and certain:

ⓒ It is likely [the value of the dollar to go up in January].
ⓓ <u>the value of the dollar</u> is likely [_____ to go up in January].

Some adjectives (like sure and apt) only allow raising with infinitives, not with "that"-clauses:

ⓔ He is sure/apt to complain about something.
ⓕ * It is sure/apt that he will complain about something.

3. Sentences That Look Like Tough Movement or Subject Raising

Some sentences look like tough movement or subject raising structures, but they are not.

ⓐ John is eager to please.

This looks like:
ⓑ John is certain to please. ← (subject raising)
ⓒ John is easy to please. ← (tough movement)

However, ⓐ is neither.

Why not subject raising?
It cannot be rephrased with a "that"-clause:

ⓓ * It is eager that John will please.
ⓔ   It is certain that John will please.

Why not tough movement?
It cannot be rephrased as:

ⓕ * It is eager to please John.
ⓖ It is easy to please John.

Also, in ⓐ, John is the subject of both clauses. He is not the object of the infinitive.

So, the correct structure is:

ⓗ John is eager to please.
ⓘ John is eager [(John) to please (someone)].

The subject of the infinitive "to please" is understood to be John, the same as the main clause subject.

• This type of sentence includes adjectives of willingness or ability, such as: able, eager, eligible, free, ready, welcome, willing.

Control Theory

Introduction

In syntactic theory, control refers to the relationship between a silent subject, called PRO, and its interpretive antecedent (the controller).

Consider the following:

- We expected to win.
- We expected [PRO to win].

Here, PRO is interpreted as referring to the subject we. This interpretive relationship, where PRO's referent is determined by another element in the sentence, is called Control. The element that determines PRO's reference is known as the controller.

Unlike movement, control does not form a syntactic chain. Instead, PRO and its controller each occupy a distinct position and receive independent theta roles from their respective predicates.

Obligatory vs. Nonobligatory Control

1. Two Interpretations of PRO

PRO can have two types of interpretations:

① Obligatory Control (OC): The reference of PRO is fixed to a specific element in the sentence.

- John wants to leave.
- John wants [PRO to leave].

→ John = controller

② Nonobligatory Control (NOC): The reference of PRO is not fixed, often understood as arbitrary or context-dependent.

- To paint like Leonardo is a common fantasy.
- [PRO to paint like Leonardo] is a common fantasy.

→ PRO = arbitrary (anyone in general)

This arbitrary PRO is often represented as PRO_{arb}.

2. PRO in Other Clause Types

Although commonly found in infinitival clauses, PRO also appears in other tenseless structures:

- John stopped [PRO crying]. → Controlled PRO
- [PRO eating] is fun. → PRO_{arb}

3. Structural Environments

To distinguish OC from NOC, we test whether a lexical subject can replace PRO.

① Obligatory Control
- John tried [PRO to understand].
- * John tried [Bill to understand].

→ PRO is required → OC

② Nonobligatory Control
- John wanted [PRO to understand].
- John wanted [Bill to understand].

→ Lexical NP possible → NOC

Infinitives with 'for' can license lexical subjects:

ⓐ [PRO to leave without John] would be hard on me, not on you.
ⓑ [For me to leave without John] would be hard on me, not on you.
ⓒ * [Me to leave without John] would be hard on me, not on you.

Sentence ⓒ is ungrammatical due to Case Filter violation. The presence of 'for' in ⓑ assigns case to the subject 'me'.

Key point: Obligatory control cannot be rescued by adding 'for'.
- * I tried [for Bill to leave]. → Still ungrammatical

Obligatory vs. Nonobligatory Control

4. Restrictions on the Controller
Both subjects and direct objects (DOs) can function as controllers.

① DO Controllers
- I persuaded Bill [PRO to leave].

→ Bill is the controller → Obligatory control

- * I persuaded Bill (for) [Mary to leave].

→ Lexical replacement not possible → OC confirmed

- [PRO to have been accused of cheating] humiliated Bill.

→ Optional PRO$_{arb}$ interpretation
→ If Bill is controller, this is Nonobligatory Control

- [For Sally to have been accused of cheating] humiliated Bill.

→ Lexical NP acceptable → NOC confirmed

② Positional Difference
In Obligatory Control, the controller must precede PRO:

- John tried [PRO to leave].
- * [PRO to leave] was tried by John.

Generalization
- Obligatory control requires that the controller linearly precede PRO.
- In Nonobligatory Control, the controller can either precede or follow PRO

5. Deleting the Controller

Another important diagnostic for distinguishing Obligatory Control (OC) from Nonobligatory Control (NOC) involves examining what happens when the controller is omitted from the sentence.

Let us revisit three examples:
ⓐ [PRO to leave without John] would be hard.
ⓑ * I persuaded [PRO to leave].
ⓒ * [PRO to have been accused of cheating] humiliated.

In example ⓐ, which corresponds to sentence '[PRO to leave without John] would be hard on me, not on you' earlier, the original sentence had an explicit controller (me) and allowed for a PROarb interpretation. After the controller is removed, the sentence remains grammatical, albeit with a generic or arbitrary interpretation of PRO. This is typical of Nonobligatory Control contexts.

However, in ⓑ and ⓒ, removing the controller (e.g., Bill in the original examples) results in ungrammatical sentences.

Why is this the case? Sentences like:

- * I persuaded.
- * That humiliated.

are ungrammatical even without an infinitival complement. These matrix verbs—persuade and humiliate—require their arguments (like a direct object) to satisfy their argument structure and valency. Thus, removing the controller from these sentences makes them ill-formed regardless of the presence of PRO.

Generalization
- In Obligatory Control, the controller is syntactically required. Removing it results in ungrammaticality.(ⓑ)
- In Nonobligatory Control, the controller is optional in terms of syntax and can often be omitted, especially when PRO is interpreted arbitrarily.(ⓐ, ⓒ)

This also helps explain why OC sentences are never ambiguous between a

Obligatory vs. Nonobligatory Control

controlled reading and a PROarb reading: the controller is necessary, so the interpretation of PRO is always fixed. In contrast, NOC sentences can be ambiguous, as they allow both specific (controlled) and arbitrary readings depending on context.

Property	Obligatory Control (OC)	Nonobligatory Control (NOC)
Interpretation of PRO	Fixed, determined by a controller	Arbitrary or context-dependent
Can lexical NP replace PRO?	X	O
Use of for + NP	Unacceptable	Acceptable
Linear order	Controller must precede PRO	Controller can follow or precede PRO
Controller deletable?	ungrammatical	Sometimes, if verb allows
Ambiguity	Never ambiguous	May be ambiguous with PROarb

Binding Theory

The Basic Concepts of Binding Theory

1. Dominance (Domination)

A node A dominates node B if:

- A is higher up in the syntactic tree than B, and
- you can trace a line from A to B going only downward.

In short, if A is above B and connected directly or indirectly by downward branches, then A dominates B.

2. C-command

C-command helps us understand how elements in a sentence relate to one another.

A node A c-commands:
- its sisters, and
- all of the daughters (and granddaughters, etc.) of its sisters.

C-command is crucial for understanding how pronouns and anaphors are interpreted.

The Basic Concepts of Binding Theory

3. Binding Principles

Binding Theory explains how different types of noun phrases (NPs) relate in terms of reference.

There are three key principles:

① Binding Principle A: Anaphors
An anaphor must:

- be bound in its binding domain.
- be locally bound (by a nearby NP).
- be c-commanded by a coindexed antecedent within the same minimal clause.

Anaphor: An NP that obligatorily gets its meaning from another NP in the sentence. → reflexives, reciprocals, etc.

② Binding Principle B: Pronouns
A pronoun must:

- be free in its binding domain.
- not be locally bound by a coindexed NP nearby(be locally free).

Pronoun (pronominal): An NP that may (but need not) get its meaning from another NP in the sentence. → he, she, him, her, etc.

③ Binding Principle C: R-expressions
An R-expression must:

- be free everywhere — it cannot be bound at all.

R-expression(Referential-expression): An NP that gets its meaning by referring to an entity in the world. → John, Brandon, Sally, etc

Coindex and Antecedent

Understanding how noun phrases (NPs) relate to one another in meaning is essential to applying Binding Theory. Two key concepts help us analyze these relationships: antecedent and coindexing.

1. Antecedent

An antecedent is a noun phrase (NP) that gives its meaning to another NP in the sentence.

Heidi$_i$ bopped herself$_i$ on the head with a zucchini.
- Here, Heidi is the antecedent of herself.
- Herself is an anaphor that depends on Heidi for its interpretation.

2. Coindexing

To show when two NPs refer to the same entity, we use indices or indexes (small subscript letters like i, j, k). If two NPs have the same index, they are said to be coindexed.

Indexing Demonstrated

[Colin]$_i$ gave [Andrea]$_j$ [a basketball]$_k$.
→ All NPs refer to different entities → each gets a different index.

[Art]$_i$ said that [he]$_j$ played [basketball]$_k$ in [the dark]$_l$.
→ He ≠ Art → different indices → he is not coindexed with Art.

[Art]$_i$ said that [he]$_i$ played [basketball]$_k$ in [the dark]$_l$.
→ He = Art → coindexed → same referent.

[Heidi]$_i$ bopped [herself]$_i$ on [the head]$_j$ with [a zucchini]$_k$.
→ Herself is coindexed with Heidi → herself = Heidi
→ This is a case of Binding Principle A (local anaphor bound by its antecedent).

Binding

While coindexation, coreference, and antecedence tell us who refers to whom in a sentence, they are not enough to account for grammaticality. For anaphors (like herself), structural conditions—specifically c-command—must also be met. This is where binding comes in.

ⓐ Heidi$_i$ bopped herself$_i$ on the head with a zucchini.
ⓑ [Heidi$_i$'s mother]$_j$ bopped herself$_j$ on the head with a zucchini.
ⓒ * [Heidi$_i$'s mother]$_j$ bopped herself$_i$ on the head with a zucchini.

In ⓐ: Heidi c-commands and is coindexed with herself → binding is satisfied
In ⓑ: Heidi's mother (as a whole NP) c-commands herself → correct local binding
In ⓒ: Heidi is embedded within the subject and does not c-command herself → violates binding

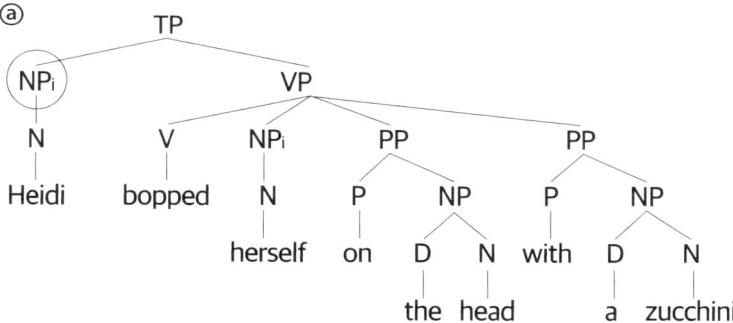

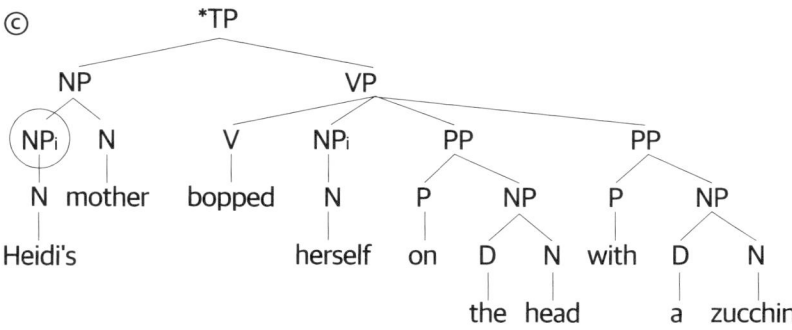

Binding

Key Definition: Binding
A binds B if and only if:

- A c-commands B
- A and B are coindexed

Binding = Coindexation + C-command

So, just being coindexed is not enough. The antecedent must also structurally dominate (c-command) the anaphor.

Violating Principle A
* Herself$_i$ bopped Heidi$_i$ on the head.
* [Heidi$_i$'s mother]$_j$ bopped herself$_i$ on the head.

In both: herself is not bound by the coindexed antecedent → violates Principle A

Binding Principle A (Preliminary Version)
→ An anaphor must be bound (i.e., coindexed with and c-commanded by its antecedent).

Locality Conditions on the Binding of Anaphors

We've learned that anaphors (like herself) must be bound—that is, coindexed and c-commanded by their antecedents. But now we add a new crucial condition: locality.

1. Unexpected Ungrammaticality

ⓐ * Heidi$_i$ said that herself$_i$ discoed with Art.
(cf. Heidi$_i$ said that she$_i$ discoed with Art.)

Structurally, Heidi c-commands and is coindexed with herself → should satisfy binding.
Yet the sentence is ungrammatical. Why?

2. The Problem: Locality
The issue is not binding, but binding within the correct domain.

In ⓐ, herself is in an embedded clause, and Heidi is in the matrix clause.

The anaphor must find its antecedent within its own clause—its binding domain.

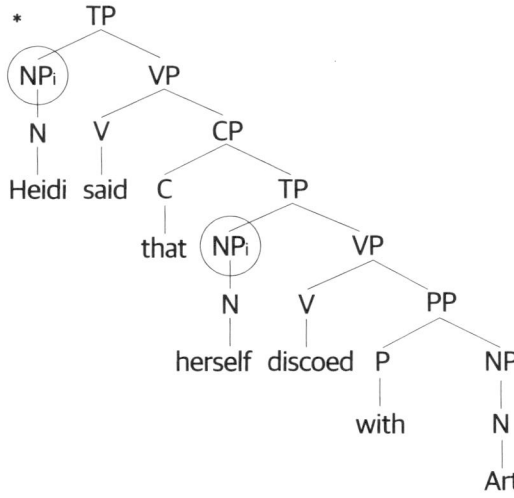

Locality Conditions on the Binding of Anaphors

3. Binding Domain

The clause (TP) containing the NP (anaphor, pronoun, or R-expression). In other words, an anaphor cannot "reach outside" its clause to find its antecedent.

4. Revision of Binding Principle A

- Binding Principle A (revised)

An anaphor must be bound within its binding domain.

This means:
- The antecedent must c-command the anaphor,
- The antecedent and anaphor must be coindexed,
- And this must all happen within the same clause.

The Distribution of Pronouns

Just like anaphors, pronouns (e.g., he, her, him) have specific syntactic restrictions on where they can appear. But unlike anaphors, their rules work in the opposite way.

1. Local Binding (Clause-Mate)

ⓐ Heidi$_i$ bopped her$_j$ on the head with the zucchini.
ⓑ * Heidi$_i$ bopped her$_i$ on the head with the zucchini.

In ⓐ, her refers to someone else ≠ Heidi
In ⓑ, her refers to Heidi, who c-commands it in the same clause → violates Binding Principle B

2. Binding Principle B

Principle B:
A pronoun must be free in its binding domain (i.e., it cannot be bound by a clause-mate antecedent).

- Free = Not Bound
- Free = Not c-commanded and coindexed within the same clause.

3. Comparison with Anaphors
- Anaphors (like herself) → must be bound in their clause (Principle A)
- Pronouns (like her) → must not be bound in their clause (Principle B)
→ They are complementary in distribution.

4. Embedded Clause Example
ⓐ Heidi$_i$ said [cp that she$_i$ discoed with Art].
ⓑ Heidi$_i$ said [cp that she$_k$ discoed with Art].

In ⓐ, she refers to Heidi → Bound, but not within the same clause → Allowed
In ⓑ, she refers to someone else → Not bound → Allowed

- Conclusion: Pronouns can be bound across clauses, but not inside the same clause as their antecedent.

The Distribution of R-Expressions

R-expressions (Referential Expressions) are noun phrases like Mary, John, Bill, Heidi, etc. They refer to entities in the real world, not to other noun phrases in the sentence.

1. Binding Principle C
- Principle C:

An R-expression must be free.

This means:
- R-expressions must not be coindexed with a c-commanding antecedent.
- This applies anywhere in the sentence (not just within the same clause).

2. Examples
- * Heidi$_i$ kissed Mary$_i$.
- * Art$_i$ kissed Geoff$_i$.
- * She$_i$ kissed Heidi$_i$.
- * She$_i$ said that Heidi$_i$ was a disco queen.

In all of these examples, the R-expression (Mary, Geoff, Heidi) is c-commanded and coindexed with a pronoun or NP earlier in the sentence.

This violates Principle C, because R-expressions must not be bound at all.

3. Why?
R-expressions get their reference from context (not from another NP in the sentence).

So,
- They must remain independent.
- They cannot corefer with a c-commanding NP (unlike pronouns or anaphors).

Case Theory

Case

1. What is Case Theory?
Case Theory explains:
- Why overt Noun Phrases (NPs) appear in certain syntactic positions.
- How NPs get their case features (e.g., nominative, accusative, genitive).
- The rules that assign abstract Case (a syntactic requirement) even when no visible morphology is present.

2. Morphological Case in English
English pronouns show different forms (morphological case) depending on their syntactic position:

Case	Example Word	Usage Example
Nominative	he	He attacked the robber. (Subject of finite clause)
Accusative	him	The butler attacked him. (Object of verb)
Genitive	his	His coat was too big. (Possessive)

3. Example Breakdown
① Clause Types
ⓐ The butler attacked the robber.
ⓑ [That the butler attacked the robber] is surprising.
ⓒ [For the butler to attack the robber] would be surprising.

② Pronoun Substitution
ⓐ He attacked him.
ⓑ That he attacked him is surprising.
ⓒ For him to attack him would be surprising.

In 2-ⓐ, "he" is the subject → nominative, "him" is the object → accusative
In (2-ⓑ), same pattern in a finite embedded clause.
In (2-ⓒ), "him" is the subject of a non-finite clause → still accusative!

4. From Morphological to Abstract Case
Traditional grammar explains this with surface forms, but generative grammar introduces:
- Abstract Case: a syntactic feature that must be licensed in certain structural positions.
- Case Assignment is structural, not just morphological:
  - Verbs and prepositions assign accusative case.
  - T (Tense) in finite clauses assigns nominative case.
  - The preposition for can also assign case to subjects of infinitival clauses.

Complements – Accusative Case Assigned by V and P in Case Theory

1. Case Assignment to Complements
- Transitive Verbs and Prepositions are Accusative Case Assigners.
- They assign accusative case to the noun phrases (NPs) they govern.

2. Examples of Case Assignment by Verbs and Prepositions

- He attacked him. → Verb assigns Accusative Case to "him"
- She walked toward him. → Preposition assigns Accusative Case to "him"

In both examples, the NP "him" gets accusative case because it is the complement of either a verb (attacked) or a preposition (toward).

3. Verbs That Cannot Assign Case: Intransitive Verbs
Intransitive verbs do not take direct objects, and therefore cannot assign accusative case:

- *He wandered them.
- *He overate them.

These are ungrammatical because there's no accusative case assigner for "them."

4. Nouns and Adjectives Cannot Assign Case Either

ⓐ *Poirot's attack him.
ⓑ *Poirot is envious him.

In ⓐ, attack is a noun, not a verb → can't assign accusative case.
In ⓑ, envious is an adjective → can't assign accusative case.

- Conclusion

Only transitive verbs and prepositions are accusative case assigners. These are the only categories that can license an NP complement with accusative case. All other categories (like intransitive verbs, nouns, and adjectives) cannot assign case, so placing an NP after them leads to ungrammaticality.

Subjects - Nominative and Accusative Case

1. Case Assignment to Subjects

There are two kinds of clauses:
- Finite clause: [+Tense, +Agreement] → assigns Nominative Case
- Non-finite clause: [-Tense, -Agreement] → does not assign Case

2. Subjects of Finite Clauses: Nominative Case

Example:
He attacked him.

- "He" is the subject in a finite clause.
- It appears in nominative case.
- Assigned by finite INFL(Inflection, I node) (Tense/Agreement node) via specifier-head agreement (not government).

3. Subjects of Infinitival Clauses: Cannot Get Case from "to"

Example:
* [Him to attack Bill] would be illegal.

- "Him" is the subject of a non-finite clause.
- Non-finite to cannot assign case → this violates the Case Filter:

- Case Filter: Every overt NP must be assigned abstract case.

Then, how to make the sentence '[Him to attack Bill] would be illegal.' Grammatical?

There are two rescue strategies
① Add "for" to assign accusative case
[For him to attack Bill] would be illegal.

"For" acts as a prepositional complementizer.
Since prepositions are accusative case assigners, it licenses "him."

② Remove the overt subject
[To attack Bill] would be illegal.

Now, there's no overt NP → no Case Filter violation.

Exceptional Case-marking (ECM)

1. What is Exceptional Case-marking (ECM)?

ECM occurs when the verb in the main clause assigns Accusative Case to the subject of its infinitival complement clause, even though that subject is not its direct object in surface structure.

Consider the sentence,
John believes [him to be a liar].

In this sentence:
"him" is the subject of the embedded to-infinitive clause ("to be a liar").

Normally, "to" cannot assign case, but every overt NP must have case (Case Filter).

So how does "him" get case?

The answer: "believe" assigns Accusative Case to "him" → this is Exceptional Case-marking.

2. ECM Structure

John believes [$_{IP}$ him to be a liar]

- The main verb believes governs into the embedded IP and assigns Case to "him".
- This is allowed because the complement is an IP, not a CP.

3. What Blocks ECM?

Consider the sentence,
* John believes for him to be a liar.

This sentence is ungrammatical because:
- "for" introduces a CP, not an IP.
- CP is a barrier for government.
- Therefore, "believe" cannot assign case to "him".

Adjectives and Nouns: of-Insertion

In English, adjectives and nouns do not assign case. Therefore, when a noun or adjective takes a complement (like a noun phrase), that NP must still receive Case in order to satisfy the Case Filter. If it doesn't, the sentence is ungrammatical. One way English deals with this is by inserting the preposition 'of', which can assign accusative case to the complement.

1. Data and Analysis

① Verbal Predicate: Case Assigned
Poirot envies Miss Marple.
- "Poirot" gets nominative case from the finite I (Infl).
- "Miss Marple" gets accusative case from the transitive verb "envy".

② Adjectival Predicate without of: No Case Assigned
* Poirot is envious Miss Marple.
- "envious" is an adjective → cannot assign case.
- "Miss Marple" receives no case → violates the Case Filter.

③ Adjectival Predicate with of: Case via 'of'
Poirot is envious of Miss Marple.
- 'of' is a preposition, and can assign accusative case to "Miss Marple".

④ Noun Phrase without 'of': No Case Assigned
* Poirot's envy Miss Marple.
- "envy" is a noun and cannot assign case.
- "Miss Marple" receives no case → violates Case Filter.

⑤ Noun Phrase with of: Case via 'of'
Poirot's envy of Miss Marple
- of assigns accusative case to "Miss Marple".

Additional Notes:
- "Poirot's" is assigned genitive case via a special functional element often labeled as POSS in [Spec, NP].
- The overall pattern is that of-insertion is required whenever an NP appears as the complement of a noun or adjective, because nouns and adjectives can't assign Case themselves.

Case Filter Reminder
- Case Filter: Every overt NP must be assigned abstract Case.
- If a noun or adjective can't assign Case, but an NP still follows it, you must insert of to satisfy the Case Filter.

Adjacency

In English, it's not enough for a verb or preposition to govern a noun phrase (NP) to assign Case. In many situations, the Case assigner (like a verb or preposition) must also be adjacent to the NP. This is called the Adjacency Requirement.

Examples and What They Show

Poirot speaks [English] fluently.
- English is a direct object of speaks, and it's adjacent to the verb.
- Verb speaks assigns accusative case to English.

* Poirot speaks fluently [English].
- Now, the adverb fluently separates the verb speaks from its NP English.
- The NP English does not receive Case → violates the Case Filter.
- This shows that adjacency matters.

Poirot sincerely believes [English to be important].
- The verb believes takes an IP complement, and case-marks English, the subject of the infinitival clause.
- Believes is adjacent to English, so case assignment works.

* Poirot believes sincerely [English to be important].
- The verb believes takes an IP complement, but believes is no longer adjacent to English (because of the adverb sincerely).
- Case cannot be assigned to English → violates the Case Filter again.

Poirot believes sincerely [that English is important].
- The clause that English is important is a finite CP.
- The subject English of the embedded clause gets Nominative Case from the finite INFL in that clause (is).
- The adjacency requirement does not apply to clauses or finite structures.

Passivization

1. Active Sentences and Case Assignment

Let's start with the following active sentence:

Italy beat Belgium in the semi-finals.

• In this sentence, all noun phrases (NPs) must receive appropriate case, according to the Case Filter (which states that every overt NP must be assigned abstract Case).
• Italy is the subject and receives nominative case from INFL (the functional element that carries tense and agreement features).
• Belgium is the object and receives accusative case from the transitive verb beat.
• Since both NPs receive the proper case, the sentence is grammatical.

2. Passive Sentences and Case Changes

Now, let's look at the passive version:

Belgium was beaten in the semi-finals.

In a passive sentence:
• The verb form changes: beat becomes the past participle beaten, and it is paired with the auxiliary be.
• The agent of the action (Italy) is not expressed as an NP in the main clause.
• If we want to include the agent, we use a by-phrase, which is an adjunct prepositional phrase (PP)

Belgium was beaten by Italy in the semi-finals.

• The subject Belgium now moves into the subject position and receives nominative case from INFL.
• The verb beaten no longer assigns accusative case, because passive verbs are assumed to absorb accusative case.

3. Ungrammatical Passives: Violating the Case Filter
Let's consider two ungrammatical sentences:

* It was beaten Belgium.
* There was beaten Belgium.

In both cases:
   • The NP Belgium is not in subject position.
   • It does not receive accusative case either, because beaten is a passive verb and cannot assign accusative case.
   • Since Belgium does not receive case, the Case Filter is violated → the sentences are ungrammatical.

4. Passivization and ECM (Exceptional Case Marking)
Let's now look at the following examples to see how case assignment works with ECM verbs (like believe) and passivization.

ⓐ   I believe [Emsworth to have attacked Poirot].

   • This is an ECM construction.
   • The verb believe assigns accusative case to the subject of the infinitival clause (Emsworth).
   • The verb attacked (active voice) assigns accusative case to its object (Poirot).

ⓑ   I believe [Poirot to have been attacked].

   • Here, attacked is in the passive voice, so there is no external argument (i.e., no agent like Emsworth is expressed).
   • Since passive verbs do not assign accusative case, Poirot must move to [Spec, IP] to get accusative case from the matrix verb believe.

Passivization

ⓒ *It was believed [Emsworth to have attcked Poirot].
                         |___ACC ↑

- In the passive, believed no longer assigns accusative case.
- Emsworth, the subject of the infinitival clause, has no source of case → this violates the Case Filter.

ⓓ It was believed [that [Emsworth had attacked Poirot]].
                      ↑ NOM |

- This is a finite clause introduced by that.
- The subject Emsworth gets nominative case from the finite INFL in the embedded clause.

The Double Object Construction

Let's now consider verbs like give, which take two internal arguments:
ⓐ I gave John a book.
ⓑ John was given a book.

1. What's Happening Here?

In sentence ⓐ, the verb give takes two objects:
- John = indirect object (the recipient)
- a book = direct object (the theme)

These are both inside the VP. But we know from Case Theory that every overt NP must receive case (according to the Case Filter).

So how are both John and a book getting case?

2. Case Assignment in ⓐ

One possible answer:
- The direct object (a book) gets ACCUSATIVE case from the verb give.
- The indirect object (John) gets inherent case (a type of case tied to meaning roles, like recipient or experiencer).

3. Evidence from Passivization

Now look at the passive version:
ⓑ John was given a book.

- John, the indirect object, becomes the subject.
- It still appears without a preposition (not to John).
- This suggests that John had inherent case, which survives passivization.

If John had only gotten ACCUSATIVE case from the verb give, it should have lost case in the passive, making the sentence ungrammatical.
But since ⓑ is grammatical, this supports the idea that John has inherent case.

Movement and Chains

In passive sentences, like the one below, we face an important question:

[IP Poirot [I' will [VP be attacked -]]].
         ↑_____NOM

1. The Visibility Problem

According to what we've learned:
- The NP Poirot gets NOMINATIVE case from the finite auxiliary will (or more precisely, from INFL).
- But Poirot is the theme (internal argument) of the verb attacked—so it also needs to receive a theta role from attacked.

But here's the issue:
- To get its theta role, Poirot must be inside the VP.
- To get its case, Poirot must move outside the VP, to subject position.

How can Poirot be in two places at once?

2. The Solution: Movement Creates a Chain

The answer lies in movement and chains. The NP Poirot:
- Starts inside the VP, as the object of attacked (where it gets its theta role).
- Then moves to the subject position (Spec-IP) to get NOMINATIVE case.

This creates a chain between the original position and the new position:
- The original position (inside VP) is now empty, marked as e.
- The moved NP and its original position are linked—they are coindexed

We represent this chain as:

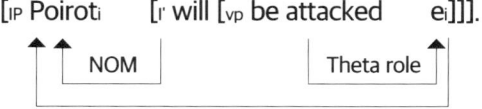

[IP Poirot$_i$ [I' will [VP be attacked e$_i$]]].

This entire chain, <Poirot$_i$, e$_i$>, receives the theta role. That's how Poirot satisfies both the Theta Criterion and the Case Filter.

Summary: Case Theory in English

We have developed a set of rules and principles to explain how Case is assigned in English sentences.

1. The Case Filter
Every overt NP must be assigned abstract Case.

This means that any NP (noun phrase) that is pronounced must have a Case, or the sentence will be ungrammatical.

2. Structural Case Assignment
Case is typically assigned by specific elements in a sentence. These are called Case-assigners.

① Case-assigners in English
- [+AGR] (finite INFL, assigns NOMINATIVE)
- V (verb, assigns ACCUSATIVE)
- P (preposition, assigns ACCUSATIVE)

② Adjacency Requirement
- Verbs and Prepositions must be adjacent to the NP they assign Case to.
- Intervening material (like adverbs) can block Case assignment.

3. Other Case Assignment Rules
In addition to structural case, English uses several other rules:

① Genitive Case Rule
An NP in [Spec, NP] gets genitive Case.
Example: [Bill's house] — Bill receives genitive Case via POSSESSOR position.

② Double-Object Rule
In double-object constructions, the second NP gets objective (accusative) Case.
Example: She gave Mary a book. → Mary gets Case from the verb.

③ Exceptional Case-Marking (ECM)
Certain verbs (e.g., believe, expect) can assign accusative Case to the subject of their infinitival complement, even across clause boundaries.
Example: I believe [him to be honest].
→ believe assigns ACC to him, even though it is the subject of the lower clause.

Grammar

Nonreferential There

1. Thematic Roles and Dummy Elements

In English, nonreferential there and expletive it are often used to fill the subject position of a sentence when no real subject (with a meaning or referent) is available.

ⓐ It always rains in London.
ⓑ There were six policemen on the bus.

In ⓐ, it is called weather it because it appears in weather-related sentences.
In ⓑ, there is called existential there because it introduces something that exists or is present.

These words do not refer to anything in the real world. Instead, they are used to fill the subject position required by English sentence structure.

By contrast:
ⓒ I hate the number 31 bus. It is always packed!
ⓓ I'll put your coffee over there.

Here, it and there refer to specific things (the bus and a place). These are referential uses.

Nonreferential There

2. What Is Nonreferential There?

English has two kinds of there:

Type	Function	Example
Deictic there	Points to a location (can be accompanied by gesture or stress)	"There is the little boy."
Nonreferential there	Fills the subject position, no specific meaning	"There is a little boy outside."

Key Differences
① Phonological and Semantic Clues
  • Deictic there is usually stressed and refers to a specific location.
  • Nonreferential there is unstressed, often reduced to [ðər], and does not refer to any place.

② Syntactic Role
  • Deictic there is an adverb. It can move around in a sentence.
  • Nonreferential there is a subject. It always stays at the beginning of the clause.

ⓐ Deictic there (movable):
"The little boy is there."

ⓑ Nonreferential there (not movable):
* "A little boy is there." → This forces a deictic (location) reading.

- Syntactic Tests for Nonreferential There

① Question Tag Test
Question tags match the subject.
"There is a little boy outside, isn't there?"
* "There's the little boy, isn't there?" (Only deictic there used incorrectly)
  - Nonreferential there can appear in the question tag.
  - Deictic there cannot.

② Negation Test
Only nonreferential there can be negated:
"There isn't a little boy outside who looks after the sheep."
* "There isn't the little boy who looks after the sheep."

③ Here Substitution Test
Deictic here can replace deictic there, but not nonreferential there:
"Here's the little boy."
* "Here's a little boy."

Pronoun

1. The Reflexives

① Reflexive Pronouns
myself, yourself, himself, herself, itself, ourselves, yourselves, themselves

② Key Properties
- Reflexive pronouns must refer back to (be coreferential with) a noun or pronoun in the same clause.
- They agree with their antecedent in person, number, and gender.

Veronica herself saw the accident. (Emphatic use)
The dog was scratching itself. (Subject = Object)
He and his wife poured themselves a drink. (Reflexive = subject group)
He and his wife poured them a drink. ('them' ≠ subject)

③ Clause Boundary Rule
Reflexives must be bound within their clause

Penelope begged Jane to look after her. → (= Penelope)
Penelope begged Jane to look after herself. → (= Jane)

④ Special Contexts
- Imperatives (understood 2nd person)

Look at yourself!

- Nonfinite clauses:

Freeing itself from the trap, the rat escaped.

⑤ Reflexives Required with Certain Verbs
Some verbs must have a reflexive if subject = object

They pride themselves.
He perjured himself.
She absented herself, behaved herself.

⑥ Optional Reflexives
With some verbs, reflexive is optional if subject = object

She dressed herself with care. = She dressed with care.
She washed, shaved, hid, prepared...

⑦ Reflexives with Prepositions
  • When the preposition is closely tied to the verb, use reflexive

Janet took a photo of herself.
She told a story about herself.

  • But when the preposition is adverbial (space, direction), reflexive is optional

Fred closed the door behind him.
→ Could be Fred or another person.
(himself would clarify the reference.)

2. Specific Reference
  • Personal Pronouns
I, you, he, she, it, we, they

  • Usually definite and have specific reference.

  • Commonly used anaphorically (referring to something already mentioned)
There's a museum. Everyone should visit it.

  • Or cataphorically (referring forward to something mentioned later)
When she had examined the patient, the doctor picked up the phone.

  • Cataphoric reference only works with subordination (like "when…").
* She examined the patient and then the doctor picked up the phone.

But you can restate it anaphorically
When the doctor had examined the patient, she picked up the phone.

Focus

1. Dislocation

① What is Dislocation?

Dislocation occurs when a noun phrase (NP) is moved to the left or right of the main clause ("nucleus") and is repeated by a pronoun inside the main clause.

- Left Dislocation (NP + Clause)

One of my cousins, she has triplets.
→ Pronoun she refers back to "One of my cousins."

- Right Dislocation (Clause + NP)

He can be very judgmental, her father.
→ Clarifies who "he" refers to.

② Why Use Dislocation?
- Left dislocation simplifies the clause by moving a complex NP to the front.
- Right dislocation helps clarify what a pronoun refers to.

Her father can be very judgmental. (Basic Sentence)
Her father, he can be very judgmental. (Left Dislocation)
He can be very judgmental, her father. (Right Dislocation)

2. Extraposition ≠ Right Dislocation

Though extraposition looks like right dislocation, they're different!

① Extraposition

It disturbs her that he was acquitted.
It remains a mystery how she escaped.

- Uses dummy subject "it".
- The real subject is postponed to the end.
- Stylistically neutral, common in both speech and writing.
- If you remove the final clause, the meaning breaks:
* It disturbs her. (What disturbs her?)

② Right Dislocation

He can be very judgmental, her father.

- Uses real pronouns, no dummy "it".
- NP at the end clarifies the pronoun.
- Informal; mostly used in speech.

3. Preposing and Postposing

① Preposing (Fronting)

Move a sentence element (especially object or adjunct) to the beginning of the sentence for emphasis or linking with previous context.

I wasn't allowed to watch TV when I was at school.
→ When I was at school, I wasn't allowed to watch TV.

I said he could have the others.
→ The others, I said he could have.

- Preposing = Fronting: No pronoun left behind
- Dislocation ≠ Fronting: Leaves behind a pronoun

② Postposing

Move a heavy (long or complex) element to the end of the clause to improve clarity and rhythm.

They brought an extraordinarily lavish lunch with them.
→ They brought with them an extraordinarily lavish lunch.

A man whom I'd never seen before came in.
→ A man came in whom I'd never seen before.

Use postposing when
- The object or modifier is long (heavy).
- It improves sentence processing and rhythm.

Structure	Use	Style	Example
Left Dislocation	Simplify nucleus / highlight NP	Informal	My uncle, he's funny.
Right Dislocation	Clarify pronoun reference	Informal	He's funny, my uncle.
Extraposition	Postpone heavy subject using "it"	Neutral	It's amazing that you finished.
Preposing (Fronting)	Emphasis or link to earlier context	Neutral-formal	This book, I love.
Postposing	Move long element to sentence end	Neutral	They brought with them a lavish lunch.

Verb Complementation

1. Clause Types: Verb Complementation Patterns

In English, verbs combine with different types and numbers of elements. These combinations are known as clause types or verb complementation patterns. Each clause type is named according to the grammatical functions that appear in the clause:

S = Subject
V = Verb
O = Object
C = Complement
A = Adverbial (typically a prepositional phrase or adverb)

Clause Type(Pattern)	Example
SV	The sun is shining.
SVO	The lecture bored me.
SVC	Your dinner seems ready.
SVA	My office is in the next building.
SVOO	I sent my parents an anniversary card.
SVOC	Most students found her helpful.
SVOA	You put the dish on the table.

2. Indirect Object and To-infinitive Clause Object

In English, certain verbs allow a structure where an indirect object is followed by a to-infinitive clause. This pattern typically expresses indirect directives—that is, when one person advises, tells, or persuades someone else to do something.

① Pattern: S + V + IO + [to-infinitive clause]

I persuaded Mark to see a doctor.
→ "Mark" is the indirect object, and to see a doctor is the to-infinitive clause (the thing being advised or persuaded).

② Passive Transformation
Only the indirect object (Mark) can become the subject in the passive version

- Active: I persuaded Mark to see a doctor.
- Passive: Mark was persuaded to see a doctor.

* To see a doctor was persuaded by me.

This shows that only the indirect object can be promoted to subject in passive constructions with this pattern.

③ Meaning and Structure
- The subject of the main verb (e.g., "I") is usually the speaker or agent giving a command, suggestion, or advice.
- The indirect object (e.g., "Mark") is the addressee or person being told to do something.
- The understood subject of the to-infinitive clause is typically the same as the indirect object:

I persuaded Mark to see a doctor = I persuaded Mark that he should see a doctor.

④ Common Verbs in This Pattern
These verbs often follow this pattern:
advise, ask, beg, command, entreat, forbid, implore, instruct, invite, order, persuade, remind, request, recommend, teach, tell, urge

> ⓐ Alternative That-clauses (Formal Register)
> In more formal styles, the to-infinitive clause can sometimes be replaced by a that-clause with a modal verb or subjunctive:
>
> I persuaded Mark to see a doctor.
> I persuaded Mark that he should see a doctor.
>
> ⓑ The Verb Promise Is Exceptional
> With promise, the subject of the to-infinitive clause is the main clause subject, not the indirect object.
>
> I promised Howard to take two shirts for his father.
> → This means: I promised Howard that I would take two shirts for his father.
>
> In contrast to persuade, where the infinitive subject is Mark, with promise, it is I.

Verb Complementation

3. Infinitival Complementation

Some English verbs can be followed by a noun phrase and a to-infinitive clause, forming patterns that look similar but differ in grammatical structure and meaning.

These structures fall into three types: Monotransitive, Ditransitive, and Complex-transitive Structures

① Monotransitive Complementation

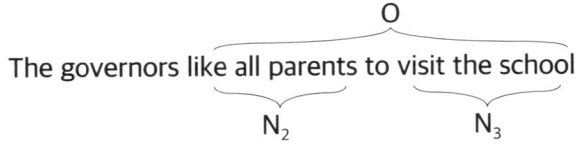

The governors like all parents to visit the school.
(N₂ = all parents, N₃ = to visit the school, O = all parents to visit the school)

In this structure, the noun phrase (N2: all parents) is part of the infinitive clause (to visit the school) and acts as the subject of that clause.

• Key Features

ⓐ The infinitive clause (including N2) can be replaced by a pronoun
The governors like all parents to visit the school, and the teachers like that too.

ⓑ The clause can be focused in a pseudo-cleft construction
What the governors like is for all parents to visit the school.

ⓒ The infinitive clause can be passivized internally
The governors like the school to be visited by all parents.

ⓓ In reduced forms, to must be retained
The governors like them to.

ⓔ Existential there can be the subject of the infinitive
We like there to be a full attendance.

② Ditransitive Complementation

I persuaded Justin to write an essay.

In this pattern, N2 (Justin) is an indirect object of the main verb (persuaded), and not part of the infinitive clause. The understood subject of the infinitive clause is the indirect object.

- Key Features

ⓐ The whole clause cannot be replaced by a pronoun
* I persuaded that

ⓑ Pseudo-cleft is not acceptable
* What I persuaded was for Justin to write an essay.

ⓒ Passive of the embedded clause is not possible
* I persuaded the essay to be written by Justin.

ⓓ The infinitive clause can be omitted
I persuaded Justin.

ⓔ The indirect object (Justin) can become the subject in a passive sentence
Justin was persuaded to write an essay.

ⓕ Contrast
* All parents were liked to visit the school. (Not acceptable)

Verb Complementation

③ Complex-transitive Complementation

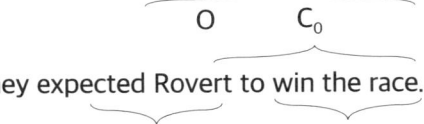

They expected Rovert to win the race.

Here, N2 (Robert) is the object of the main verb, and also the subject of the infinitive clause.

- Key Features

Similar to monotransitive verbs, the whole clause behaves like a unit

Robert was expected to win the race.
They expected the prize to be won by Robert.
The prize was expected to be won by Robert.

Thus, the object N2 can move to subject position in the passive (like ditransitive verbs), but the infinitive clause retains the internal structure of monotransitive verbs.

Determiners

1. Order of Determiners in Noun Phrases

In English, determiners are words that come at the beginning of noun phrases to provide information such as definiteness, quantity, number, and ownership.

① Three Classes of Determiners

According to Quirk et al., determiners fall into three main categories:

Pre-determiners	Central determiners	Post-determiners
all, both, half, double, three-fourths, once, twice	the, a/an, this, these, that, those, each, every, some, any, either, neither, which, whose, my, your, John's	many, much, few, little, more, most, one, two, three, first, second, next, last, another

These classes follow a fixed order in English noun phrases. That is, when multiple determiners appear in a noun phrase, they must appear in this order:

- Pre-determiner + Central determiner + Post-determiner + Noun

② Correct Examples of Determiner Order
- all the five boys
(Pre-determiner + Central determiner + Post-determiner)
- double the quantity
(Pre-determiner + Central determiner)
- all three boys
(Pre-determiner + Post-determiner)
- the second occasion
(Central determiner + Post-determiner)

③ Incorrect Orders

The following combinations are ungrammatical because they violate the fixed ordering of determiner types:

* five the all boys
(Post-determiner + Central + Pre-determiner — incorrect order)
* the all five boys
(Central + Pre-determiner + Post-determiner — incorrect order)
* the this book
(Central + Central — two items from the same category can't co-occur)

Determiners

2. Genitive Meanings

The genitive (also called the possessive form) usually appears with 's or of constructions and expresses a variety of meanings. These meanings can be understood through paraphrasing.

Below are the main types of genitive meanings, along with examples and their paraphrases:

① Possessive Genitive
This is the most basic meaning — ownership or possession.

Mrs Johnson's coat → Mrs Johnson owns this coat.
The ship's funnel → The ship has a funnel.

② Genitive of Attribute
This genitive expresses a quality or characteristic of the noun.

The victim's outstanding courage → The victim was very courageous.

③ Partitive Genitive
This genitive shows that the noun is a part of a whole.

The heart's two ventricles → The heart contains two ventricles.

④ Subjective Genitive
Here, the genitive noun performs the action described by the head noun.

The parents' consent → The parents consented.

⑤ Objective Genitive
In this case, the genitive noun receives the action expressed by the head noun.

The prisoner's release → (Someone) released the prisoner.

⑥ Genitive of Origin
This genitive shows where something comes from — a person or place of origin.

Mother's letter → The letter is from Mother.
England's cheeses → The cheeses were produced in England.

⑦ Descriptive Genitive
This genitive describes the type or purpose of the noun. It often acts like an adjective.

Children's shoes → The shoes are designed for children.
A doctor's degree → The degree is a doctorate.

3. The Grammatical Status of the Genitive

Genitive constructions (like Joan's book or the girl's coat) can have two different grammatical roles: either as a determiner or as a modifier. Let's explore both.

① Genitive as a Determiner
Most of the time, genitives behave just like central determiners such as the, this, or my. That means:
- They appear at the beginning of the noun phrase, and
- They don't usually allow another determiner to appear before them.

A new briefcase
The new briefcase
This new briefcase
Joan's new briefcase

* A the new briefcase
* The this new briefcase
* The Joan's new briefcase

Even when the genitive phrase includes its own determiner, it still acts as a single determiner for the entire noun phrase:

My cousin's new briefcase
My handsome cousin's new briefcase

Here, the genitive (e.g., my cousin's) works like a determiner, so no other determiner (like the or a) can be added before it.

- Exception: Predeterminers

Determiners

There is one exception to the rule above — when a predeterminer (like both) is used. In this case, both can refer either to:

ⓐ the genitive noun:
We attributed both the girls' success to their hard work.
→ (both modifies the girls, meaning "the success of both the girls")

ⓑ the head noun:
Both the girl's parents were present.
→ (both modifies the parents, meaning "both the parents of the girl")

② Genitive as a Modifier
Sometimes the genitive does not act like a determiner, but rather like a modifier. In this case, it classifies the noun that comes after it — like an adjective.

Here, the genitive does not block other determiners from appearing in the phrase.

They attend a women's university in Kyoto.
→ Women's is not the determiner; it is a modifier that tells us what kind of university it is.
→ The actual determiner is a, which goes with university, not women's.

You can tell this is true because a (which is singular) would never appear with women (which is plural) unless women's is a modifier, not a determiner.

4. Definite Articles in Discourse

In English, the choice between using 'a(n)' and 'the' often depends on the discourse context—that is, what the speaker and listener know or have already mentioned.

Let's explore five key situations where the definite article the is used.

① First vs. Second Mention of a Noun
When a noun is mentioned for the first time, we usually use a(n). But when we refer to it again, we use the to show that we are talking about the same thing.

First mention: She has a brother and a sister.
Second mention: The brother is a university student. The sister is still in high school.

This is called the anaphoric use of "the" — we refer back to something already mentioned.

However, if we use a again in the second sentence, we're not referring to the same people:

A brother can either be a good friend... → This refers to any brother in general.

② Referring to Objects in the Immediate Environment
We use the when both the speaker and the listener know what object is being referred to—especially if it's visible or present in the situation.

"Pass the butter, please."
→ The butter is clearly on the table, visible to both speaker and listener.

Even if we don't see the object but know it's there (like at the zoo), we still use the:
"Do not feed the bears."

③ Referring to Shared Knowledge in a Larger Context
Speakers also use the when talking about something that is common knowledge within a community, workplace, or other shared setting.

"Let's meet at the cafeteria at 12:15."
→ Both speakers likely work at the same place and know which cafeteria is meant.

Determiners

④ Knowledge of Relationships Between Things
This use is called associative anaphora. Even if something hasn't been mentioned yet, we use the if it is logically or culturally connected to something else that has.

"An SUV was involved in an accident on the freeway. The driver and the passengers were injured."
→ Even though this is the first mention of the driver and passengers, we expect an SUV to have them, so the is used.

Also, the freeway assumes the listener knows which freeway is being talked about (from shared context or experience).

⑤ Generic Reference
When we talk about an entire group or species, we're using generic reference. English has three ways to do this:
- Zero article + plural noun
Tigers are dangerous animals.

- A(n) + singular noun
A tiger is a dangerous animal.

- The + singular noun
The tiger is a dangerous animal.

This third pattern is more formal and commonly used in academic writing (e.g., biology textbooks: "The howler monkey is found in Central America").

Stative and Dynamic Senses of Verbs

1. Stative and Dynamic Verbs

Verbs describe different types of situations. These situations can be classified into two main types: stative and dynamic.

① Stative verbs describe a state or condition that is continuous and unchanging.

Examples: be, have, know
I have known the Penfolds all my life.

② Dynamic verbs describe actions, events, or processes that involve change or activity.

Examples: drive, speak, attack
I have driven sports cars for years.

- Shift in Verb Meaning

Some verbs can have both stative and dynamic meanings depending on the context.

ⓐ She has two sisters. → stative
ⓑ We have dinner at Maxim's quite frequently. → dynamic

- Tests for Dynamic Verbs

Only dynamic verbs can:

ⓐ Be used in the imperative:
Learn how to swim. / * Know how to swim.

ⓑ Occur in the progressive form:
I am learning to swim. / * I am knowing how to swim.

ⓒ Follow do in pseudo-cleft constructions:
What she did was learn Spanish./ * What she did was know Spanish.

Stative and Dynamic Senses of Verbs

2. Simple Past Tense for Past Time

The simple past expresses situations that happened at a specific, definite time in the past.

① Event Past (with dynamic verbs)
• Refers to a single past event:
The Normans invaded England in 1066.
The plane left at 9 a.m.

② Habitual Past (with dynamic verbs)
• Refers to repeated past actions:
We spent our holidays in Spain when we were children.

③ State Past (with stative verbs)
• Refers to an unbroken state in the past:
I once liked reading novels.

3. The Present Perfect

The present perfect describes situations that occurred at an indefinite time in the past, within a time frame that extends to the present.

① State Present Perfect (with stative verbs)
• Refers to a state that started in the past and continues now (and possibly into the future):
We have lived in Amsterdam for five years.
She has owned the house since her father died.

② Event Present Perfect (with dynamic verbs)
• Describes one or more past events within a time period leading to the present. There are two subtypes:

ⓐ Recent events reported as news:
The Republicans have won the election.
I've just got a new job.
There's been a serious accident.

ⓑ Events from the past still relevant now:
She has given an interview only once in her life. (She may give another.)
Have you seen the new production of King Lear? (You can still see it.)

③ Habitual Present Perfect (with dynamic verbs)
• Describes repeated actions from the past up to the present:

The magazine has been published every month (since 1975).
I've been reading only science fiction (till now).
Socrates has influenced many philosophers (till now).

Present Perfect vs. Simple Past

- The present perfect does not go with adverbials that refer to a specific past time:

* I have seen her a week ago.
 I saw her a week ago.

- The present perfect is used with adverbials that refer to a period extending to the present, such as:

since (e.g., since Monday, since I met you)
till now, up to now, so far

Modal Auxiliaries

Modal auxiliaries (e.g., must, may, can, should, will, dare) express meanings related to possibility, necessity, permission, obligation, and ability. These meanings fall into three main categories: epistemic, deontic, and dynamic.

1. The Epistemic vs. Deontic Contrast

① Epistemic Modality
 • Refers to knowledge, belief, or inference.
 • Expresses how certain the speaker is that something is true or likely to be true.
 • Based on evidence, reasoning, or lack of information.

Example:
He must have overslept. (I infer this from the situation.)

② Deontic Modality
 • Refers to rules, obligations, or permissions.
 • Expresses what is required, allowed, or forbidden.
 • Based on authority, norms, or what's considered the right thing to do.

Example:
He must apologize. (There is an obligation.)

Compare the Pairs:

Sentence	Epistemic Meaning	Deontic Meaning
(i) a. He must have overslept.	I infer that he did.	—
(i) b. He must apologize.	—	He is obliged to.
(ii) a. She may be ill.	It's possible she's ill.	—
(ii) b. She may take as many as she needs.	—	She has permission.
(iii) a. The storm should be over soon.	It's expected to be over.	—
(iii) b. We should call the police.	—	It's the right thing to do.

2. Modal Ambiguity

Some sentences can be interpreted both epistemically and deontically, depending on context:

You must be very tactful.

- Epistemic: I believe you are very tactful.
- Deontic: You are expected to behave tactfully.

Key Difference:
- Epistemic modality = truth/likelihood of a situation.
- Deontic modality = necessity or permission to act.

3. Dynamic Interpretations

Dynamic modality deals with personal abilities, volition (willingness), or internal states of individuals.

Examples:

Sentence	Dynamic Meaning
She can speak five languages.	She has the ability.
He won't help us.	He refuses to help (unwillingness).
I daren't tell you any more.	I lack the courage.

Note: Dare is unique in that it only has a dynamic use.

Modal Auxiliaries

4. Dynamic vs. Epistemic/Deontic Ambiguity

Some modals (especially can) can have more than one interpretation:

ⓐ You can't be serious.
- Epistemic: I believe it's impossible that you're serious.
- Dynamic: You are incapable of being serious (your personality).

ⓑ She can drive.
- Deontic: She has permission to drive.
- Dynamic: She has the ability to drive.

Summary of the Three Modal Types

Modal Meaning	Definition	Example
Epistemic	Related to knowledge, inference, or belief	She must be at home now.
Deontic	Related to rules, duties, and permissions	You must wear a helmet.
Dynamic	Related to ability, volition, or inner capacity	He can lift heavy weights.

Negation

1. Negative and Positive Polarity Items

In English, certain words behave differently depending on whether a sentence is affirmative (positive) or negative. These words are called polarity items.

① Positive Polarity Items (PPIs)
Words like some, somebody, still, and too are known as positive polarity items. These are generally used in affirmative (positive) sentences and often become incorrect when used in a negative context.

There are some crows in the tree.
* There aren't some crows in the tree.
Her mother is coming too.
* Her mother isn't coming too.

To correct the negative versions, we use nonassertive forms:

There aren't any crows in the tree.
Her mother isn't coming either.

② Negative Polarity Items (NPIs)
Words like any, anybody, ever, yet, and at all are known as negative polarity items. These words usually appear only in negative sentences or other negative-like contexts.

She doesn't have any money.
* She has any money.

In the first sentence, any appears naturally after the negative verb "doesn't." In the second, it sounds incorrect because any is being used in a positive sentence — it violates the rules of polarity.

• Assertive vs. Nonassertive Forms

Here's a chart to help compare positive (assertive) and negative (nonassertive) versions:

Assertive (Positive)	Nonassertive (Negative)
We've had some lunch.	We haven't had any lunch.
I spoke to somebody.	I didn't speak to anybody.
They will finish it somehow.	They won't finish it at all.
He sometimes visits us.	He doesn't ever visit us.
He's still at school.	He's not at school any longer.
She's coming too.	She's not coming either.
I like her a great deal.	I don't like her much.

Negation

2. Syntactic Features of Clause Negation

Negative clauses in English are not just different in meaning — they also show clear syntactic (structural) differences from positive clauses. Below are several important features that make negative clauses unique.

① Negative Clauses Use Positive Tag Questions
When a sentence is negative, it is usually followed by a positive question tag.

They aren't ready, are they?
(Compare with the positive sentence: They are ready, aren't they?)

This pattern helps confirm or check information, and the contrast between negative main clause + positive tag is a key syntactic pattern.

② Negative Clauses Can Be Followed by 'Negative Tag Clauses'
Negative clauses can be followed by additive tag clauses like and neither – auxiliary + subject or and nor + auxiliary + subject.

They aren't ready, and neither are you.

This structure adds another negative clause in a concise way.

③ Negative Clauses Allow Negative Agreement Responses
When someone says a negative sentence, the reply often agrees with the negation using a structure like:

A: He doesn't know Russian.
B: No, he doesn't.

These kinds of negative agreement responses are common in dialogue and help reinforce or confirm a negative statement.

④ Negative Clauses Are Followed by Nonassertive Items
As explained, nonassertive items like any, ever, either, and much typically appear only in negative clauses.

He won't notice any change in you, either.

This sentence uses any and either, which are nonassertive forms that appear naturally in the negative environment created by won't.

3. Tag Questions

In English, a tag question is a short question added to the end of a sentence. It is often used to confirm information or seek agreement from the listener.

One common type is called the reversed polarity tag question, where the main clause and the tag have opposite polarity:

- If the main sentence is positive, the tag is negative.
- If the main sentence is negative, the tag is positive.

Let's look at both cases:

① Positive Sentence + Negative Tag
These tag questions start with an affirmative (positive) main clause and end with a contracted negative tag.

He likes football, doesn't he?
She can come, can't she?
He is helping her, isn't he?
She is a doctor, isn't she?

These are the most common type of tag questions in everyday English. The auxiliary verb (or modal) in the tag matches the verb in the main clause.

② Negative Sentence + Positive Tag
When the main clause is negative, the tag becomes positive. Notice that these negative sentences usually contain contractions like doesn't, can't, or isn't.

He doesn't like football, does he?
She can't come, can she?
He isn't helping her, is he?
She isn't a doctor, is she?

Negation

4. The Types of Negation

Negation in English can occur at three different structural levels: lexical, phrasal, and sentential. Understanding the difference is important for identifying how much of the sentence is being negated and how it affects meaning.

① Lexical Negation
Lexical negation happens within a single word. This means that a negative prefix is added to a word, often an adjective or a verb.

Harry is uncoordinated, isn't he?

- The word uncoordinated is lexically negated (by the prefix un-).
- The sentence as a whole is still affirmative, which is why the tag question is negative (isn't he?).

② Phrasal Negation
Phrasal negation occurs when the word not negates a verb phrase rather than the entire sentence.

Marge has decided not to pay her taxes, hasn't she?

- The negation not applies only to the infinitive phrase (to pay her taxes), not to the entire sentence.
- The sentence as a whole is affirmative, which is why the tag question is negative (hasn't she?).

③ Sentential Negation
Sentential negation negates the entire proposition or meaning of the sentence.

John is not at home, is he?

- The word not directly negates the main verb of the sentence.
- Because the sentence is negative, the tag question is affirmative (is he?).

This is the most common and most powerful form of negation in English, affecting the whole meaning of the sentence.

Using Tag Questions to Test Negation Type

A useful way to test the scope of negation is by adding a tag question:
- If the tag is negative, the sentence is affirmative.
- If the tag is positive, the sentence is negative.

Scope of no and Related Negatives

Even though no is technically just a determiner, it can function as if it has sentential scope.

No one came to fix the plumbing, did they?
Nothing is going right, is it?
They never answered, did they?

In each of these, the entire sentence is interpreted as negative, which is shown by the affirmative tag (did they?, is it?).

Negation

5. Changes in the Relative Scope of Negation

In English, the position of the negative word "not" and other elements like adverbs can affect what part of the sentence is being negated. This is called a change in the scope of negation.

① What Is Scope of Negation?
The scope of negation refers to how much of the sentence is being negated or which part the word "not" affects.

② Full Sentence Negation
In some cases, the entire meaning of the sentence is negated.

ⓐ Tom did not destroy the evidence.
ⓑ Tom destroyed the evidence.

In ⓐ, not negates the whole sentence.
It means that the action of destroying the evidence did not happen.

③ Scope Changes with Adverbs
When certain adverbs (like deliberately, knowingly, on purpose, expressly, intentionally, willfully, purposely) are added, the meaning can change depending on where the adverb appears in the sentence.

Let's look at two examples with different adverb positions:

Example 1
She expressly did not withhold information from the police.

- Here, not negates the verb withhold.
- This means: she didn't withhold information.(She did give the police the information.)
- The adverb expressly (meaning clearly or specifically) emphasizes the intention not to withhold information.

Example 2
She did not expressly withhold information from the police.

- Here, the not negates the adverb expressly, not the verb withhold.
- This means: She did withhold the information, but not on purpose or not clearly/intentionally.

6. Negative Constituents and C-command: Syntactic Restrictions

In English, certain words—called Negative Polarity Items (NPIs)—can only appear in negative environments. One such word is ever.

① When Can You Use Ever?
The word ever cannot appear in a regular, positive sentence:

* I will ever forgive you for that.
Nobody will ever forgive you for that.
I won't ever forgive you for that.

② But Not All Negative Sentences Allow Ever
Sometimes a sentence looks negative, but it still does not allow the use of ever.

* I will ever forgive nobody for that.
* Someone who didn't like you would ever forgive you for that.

Even though these sentences contain negative expressions like nobody or didn't, ever is not allowed. Why?

• Syntactic Explanation: C-command and Licensing
To understand this, we use a syntactic principle called C-command. Here's the basic idea:
For ever to be licensed, it must be c-commanded by a negative element like not, no, or nobody.

I won't ever forgive you.
  • won't is a negative auxiliary and c-commands ever.
  • Both are under the same S (sentence), so ever is licensed.

* Someone who didn't like you would ever forgive you.
  • The negative word didn't is inside a relative clause and does not c-command ever.
  • So, ever is not licensed here.

Passive

1. Semantic Constraints on Using the Passive

In English, the passive voice is formed by using a form of "be" + past participle, and is generally used with transitive verbs—verbs that take a direct object.

However, not every passive sentence with a transitive verb is acceptable. The acceptability depends on several semantic factors. Let's explore them.

① Definiteness of the Subject
The more definite (specific or known) the subject of a passive sentence is, the more natural the sentence sounds.

- Acceptable

This poem was written by Henry Wadsworth Longfellow.
- Less acceptable

Poems were written by Henry Wadsworth Longfellow.

In English, the subject usually carries given or known information, so when the subject is indefinite (like "poems"), the passive can sound awkward or vague.

② Indefiniteness of the Agent (by-phrase)
With stative verbs (like like, love, know), passive sentences are more acceptable when the agent in the by-phrase is indefinite.

- Acceptable

Arthur Ashe was liked by everybody.
The movie has been seen by everyone in town.
- Less acceptable

Arthur Ashe was liked by me.
The movie has been seen by Jim.

Using general or indefinite agents makes the passive more natural, especially with stative verbs.

③ Type of Verb: Action vs. State
The more the verb expresses a physical action, the more natural it sounds in the passive. Verbs that describe states or conditions are less likely to appear in passive sentences.

- Acceptable

The ball was kicked over the goalposts.
- Less acceptable

The ball was wanted by the other team.

However, even stative verbs like want can sound okay in passive voice if the subject is indefinite or fits well in context:

This old jalopy of mine must be wanted by somebody.

④ Verbs That Generally Do NOT Work in Passive
Some transitive verbs almost never occur in passive voice, especially when they describe states or non-actions. These include:

- Verbs of Containing(contain, hold, comprise)
* Two gallons of water are held by the watering can.

- Verbs of Measure(weigh, cost, contain, last)
* Five dollars is cost by the parking fine.

- Reciprocal Verbs(resemble, loo k like, equal)
* Lori is resembled by her father.

- Verbs of Fitting(fit, suit)
* He is suited by the plan.

- Verbs of Possession(have, belong)
* A car is had by him.

Passive

2. Passive Look-Alikes: Pseudo-Passive / Stative Passive

Sometimes, a sentence that looks like it's in the passive voice actually isn't. These sentences use be + past participle, but the past participle is functioning not as part of a passive verb form, but as a participial adjective.

Consider the example,

The library is located on the other side of the campus.

At first glance, this might seem like a short passive sentence. But it's not actually passive. The verb locate is not being used in a passive construction here—it's being used as an adjective that describes the state or condition of the library (its location).

① Can We Make It Active?
A good test for passives is to try and turn them into active sentences. Let's test that with the sentence above.

Someone locates the library on the other side of the campus.

This sentence sounds strange and doesn't carry the same meaning. That's because the original sentence is not a passive, but a stative sentence using a participial adjective.

② What Is a Stative Passive?
This type of sentence is sometimes called a stative passive, because it expresses a state or condition rather than an action. But this name can be confusing, because these aren't really passive sentences at all. Instead, the past participle functions just like an adjective after be.

He was frightened.
She was amazed.

These aren't actions being done to someone—they are describing how someone felt.

③ How to Tell the Difference: Use Adverbs!
Participial adjectives can often be modified by degree adverbs like:
very, too, quite, somewhat, a little

If you can add one of these before the past participle, it's probably a participial adjective (not a passive verb).

The student was very motivated. (Adjective)
* The essay was very written. (Passive verb + adverb? Doesn't work!)

So, if it sounds natural with "very," it's probably not a true passive.

④ Ambiguous Cases
Some sentences can be ambiguous—they may have two interpretations: one adjectival, the other passive.

The shop is closed at five o'clock.

- Adjectival meaning: The shop is in a closed state at 5:00.
- Passive meaning: Someone closes the shop at 5:00.

In these cases, context helps you decide.

- Context Test Example

When Mrs. Dalyrimple walked into the room, she saw that the vase was smashed. It lay in a thousand pieces on the floor next to the table.
- Adjectival: Describes the condition of the vase.

In the struggle between the thief and Mrs. Dalyrimple, the vase was smashed into a thousand pieces.
- Passive: Describes the action of smashing the vase.

Passive

3. Get Passive Look-Alikes

Just like with be passives, some sentences using get + past participle may look like passives but are not really passive. These are called get passive look-alikes.

① What Are Get Passive Look-Alikes?
These are sentences where get means "become", and the past participle is actually an adjective describing a state or condition.

His explanation is getting complicated.

- This sentence looks like a passive, but it actually means:

His explanation is becoming complicated.

- The verb get here means "come into a state" and is not a true passive.

② How to Tell If It's NOT a Passive (Tests)

- Test 1: Can it be changed into an active sentence?

If a sentence is truly passive, you can usually turn it into an active sentence by adding a subject (the doer).

ⓐ He got stuck in the elevator.
ⓑ Someone stuck him in the elevator.

Since you can't rewrite ⓐ into a natural active sentence(ⓑ), it's not a real passive. It's a get + adjective construction.

- Test 2: Can you add "becoming" adverbs?

If get means "become," you can often insert adverbs like:
more and more
gradually
less and less
very / somewhat / a little

ⓐ Education is getting specialized.
ⓑ Education is getting more and more specialized.
Since ⓑ is grammatical, we know specialized is an adjective.

ⓒ We're getting paid. (Passive)
ⓓ We're getting more and more paid.
This is ungrammatical, which shows ⓒ is a real passive.

③ Common Participial Adjectives with Get
These adjectives are frequently used with get in the "become" sense:
alarmed, complicated, depressed, interested, lost, tired, worried

She got worried.
She got a little worried.

The fact that we can add "a little" shows that this is not passive, but a get + adjective structure.

④ Ambiguous Cases
Sometimes, the sentence can have two meanings:

ⓐ They got very frightened.
- Likely: They became frightened (adjective meaning)
ⓑ They got frightened out of their wits by a bunch of skinheads.
- Passive: Someone frightened them...

The context helps us decide whether the sentence is a passive or a get + adjective.

- Get + Regular Adjectives

Get is also commonly used with ordinary adjectives (not participles) to mean "become":
angry, anxious, busy, cold, hungry, old, etc.

It suddenly got cold. = It suddenly became cold.

Relative Clauses

1. Restrictive vs. Nonrestrictive Relative Clauses

English relative clauses are divided into two main types: restrictive and nonrestrictive, depending on their function in the sentence.

① Restrictive Relative Clauses
A restrictive relative clause gives essential information about the noun it modifies. It restricts or limits the meaning of the noun, helping the reader or listener know exactly which person or thing is meant.

My sister who lives in Canada is a biologist.

- In this sentence, the clause 'who lives in Canada' restricts the meaning of my sister.
- It tells us which sister the speaker is talking about (the one in Canada).
- This implies that the speaker has more than one sister, and only one of them is a biologist.
- This could be used to answer the question: Which of your sisters is a biologist?

② Nonrestrictive Relative Clauses
A nonrestrictive relative clause adds extra information about the noun. This information is not essential to identify the noun, because we already know who or what is being talked about.

My sister, who lives in Canada, is a biologist.

- In this sentence, the clause 'who lives in Canada' is just additiona information.
- It doesn't help us identify which sister, because the speaker is talking about one known sister.
- This means the speaker probably has only one sister, and she happens to live in Canada.

- In writing, nonrestrictive relative clauses are set off by commas.
- They reflect the pauses we make in speech.

③ Intonation Differences in Speech
The difference between the two types is also heard in intonation

ⓐ Restrictive Relative Clause Intonation
The students who had to take finals today are tired.

- There is no pause before or after the clause.
- Falling intonation happens only at the end of the sentence, not the clause.

ⓑ Nonrestrictive Relative Clause Intonation
The students, who had to take finals, are tired.

- There is a pause before and after the clause.
- There is falling intonation at the end of the relative clause.

Relative Clauses

2. Form Criteria for Distinguishing Nonrestrictive and Restrictive Relative Clauses

To tell the difference between nonrestrictive and restrictive relative clauses, we can look at their form—how they are written and spoken. Below are seven important criteria to help identify each type.

① Use of that as a Relative Pronoun
 · Nonrestrictive clauses cannot use that as a relative pronoun.
 · Restrictive clauses can use that.

* The plan, that we discussed yesterday, will be adopted.
The plan that we discussed yesterday will be adopted.

② Stacking Relative Clauses
 · You cannot stack (combine) nonrestrictive clauses.
 · You can stack restrictive clauses.

* They gave the job to Rob, who is very qualified, who starts next month.
I really like that car that you have that your wife is always zipping around town in.

③ Sentence Modification
 · Nonrestrictive clauses can modify entire sentences, adding a comment on the whole clause.
 · Restrictive clauses can only modify noun phrases.

Professor Fish gave everyone an A, which was just fine with Alice.
* Professor Fish gave everyone an A which was just fine with Alice.

④ Modification of Words like any, every, no
 · Nonrestrictive clauses cannot modify indefinite words like any, every, or no.
 · Restrictive clauses can.

* Any man, who goes back on his word, is no friend of mine.
Any man who goes back on his word is no friend of mine.

⑤ Modification of Proper Nouns
 · Nonrestrictive clauses can modify proper nouns.
 · Restrictive clauses cannot modify proper nouns.

John, who is a linguist, was not impressed by Professor Fish's arguments.
* John who is a linguist was not impressed by Professor Fish's arguments.

⑥ Intonation (in Speech)
In nonrestrictive clauses, there is a pause before and after the clause, and the intonation falls at the end of the clause.
In restrictive clauses, there is no special pause, and falling intonation happens only at the end of the full sentence.

- Nonrestrictive:

The students, who had to take final exams today, are tired.
- Restrictive:

The students who had to take final exams today are tired.

⑦ Punctuation
- Nonrestrictive relative clauses are set off with commas.
- Restrictive relative clauses have no commas.

My sister, who lives in Canada, is a biologist.
(Nonrestrictive — adds extra info)
My sister who lives in Canada is a biologist.
(Restrictive — tells which sister)

Coordination

1. Combinatory and Segregatory Coordination of Noun Phrases

When two noun phrases are connected using and, the coordination can have two different meanings:

① Segregatory Coordination
 • The two noun phrases are treated separately.
 • You can paraphrase the sentence using two separate clauses, each with one of the nouns.
 • This type of coordination shows that each person or thing does the action individually.

John and Mary know the answer.
= John knows the answer, and Mary knows the answer.

② Combinatory Coordination
 • The two noun phrases act together as one unit.
 • You cannot paraphrase the sentence by separating the subjects.
 • This type shows that the meaning depends on their combination.

John and Mary make a pleasant couple.
≠ John makes a pleasant couple, and Mary makes a pleasant couple.

Ambiguous Example:
Some sentences can have both interpretations—either separately or together

John and Mary won a prize.
 • They each won a prize (segregatory)
 • They won one prize together (combinatory)
(Restrictive — tells which sister)

 • More Examples of Combinatory Coordination
These examples clearly show that the two noun phrases work together:
John and Mary played as partners in tennis against Susan and Bill.
Peter and Bob separated (from each other).
Paula and her brother look alike.
Mary and Paul are just good friends.
John and Peter have different tastes (from each other).
Mary and Susan are colleagues (of each other).
Law and order is a primary concern of the new administration.

2. Indicators of Segregatory Meaning

Sometimes, we want to make it clear that two or more people did something separately. This is called segregatory coordination. Certain words or phrases help us show this clearly and remove any possible ambiguity.

① Common Indicators of Segregatory Meaning

Marker	Use	Example
both A and B	Shows two people did something separately	Both John and Mary have won a prize.
each	Shows individual actions	John and Mary have each won a prize.
apiece	Means "for each person"	John and Mary have won a prize apiece.
neither A nor B	Negative segregatory meaning	Neither John nor Mary won a prize.
respective / respectively	Match things in two parallel groups	John and Peter visited their respective uncles. John and Peter ordered tea and coffee, respectively.

② Using Respective (Adjective)
respective shows a one-to-one relationship between two sets of people or things.

Jill and Ben visited their respective uncles.
→ Jill visited her uncle(s), Ben visited his uncle(s).

Without respective, this could also mean they visited uncles together.

Bob and his best friend have had trouble at school.
Their respective parents will talk to the principal.
→ Bob's parents and his friend's parents, separately.

③ Using Respectively (Adverb)
respectively links items in one list to items in another list in the same order.

John, Peter, and Robert play football, basketball, and baseball, respectively.
→ John plays football, Peter plays basketball, Robert plays baseball.

Thomas Arnold and his son Matthew were respectively the greatest educator and the greatest critic of the Victorian age.
→ Thomas = educator, Matthew = critic.

Coordination

3. Coordination within Noun Phrases

① Coordinated Noun Heads

When noun heads are coordinated (i.e., two nouns share the same determiner, modifier, or postmodifier), the usual interpretation is distributive:

The determiner, adjective, and modifier apply separately to each noun.

- his wife and child = his wife and his child
- old men and women = old men and old women
- some cows and pigs from our farm = some cows from our farm and some pigs from our farm
- the boys and girls staying at the hostel = the boys staying at the hostel and the girls staying at the hostel

Sometimes, ambiguity can occur.

old men and old women, or old men and women
some cows and pigs from our farm, or pigs from our farm and some cows

② Coordinated Modifiers

When modifiers (like adjectives or prepositional phrases) are coordinated:

- If the adjectives describe mutually exclusive traits, only segregatory (separate) meaning is allowed

old and new furniture = old furniture and new furniture
workers from France and from Italy = workers from France and workers from Italy

- Exception - Color adjectives can allow combinatory reading

red, white, and blue flags = flags that are part red, part white, part blue

- If the head noun is singular, only combinatory meaning is possible

a dishonest and lazy student = a student who is both dishonest and lazy
a book on reptiles and amphibians = a single book about both reptiles and amphibians

- The same meaning applies when the coordination is asyndetic (no 'and')

a dishonest, lazy student = one student with both qualities

- Ambiguity Cases:

Some coordinated modifiers can be ambiguous, depending on context:

old and valuable books
- books that are both old and valuable
- old books and valuable books

buses for the Houses of Parliament and for Victoria Station
- buses to both places
- separate buses to each place

- Coordination of Determiners

these and those chairs = awkward
→ Preferred: these chairs and those

your and my problems = awkward
→ Preferred: your problems and mine

- Cardinal Numbers with "or"

This is an idiomatic way to express approximation:

one or two guests = a small number of guests
five or six letters = approximately 5 or 6 letters
ten or twenty students = a number in the range of 10 to 20

Coordination

4. Coordination: Category vs. Function

For a coordination (X and Y) to be grammatically correct, the two coordinated elements must serve the same function, even if they are not the same category.

① When Coordination Is Not Allowed
These examples are ungrammatical because the two coordinated parts are very different in kind:

ⓐ * We invited [the Smiths and because they can speak Italian]
ⓑ * She argued [persuasively or that their offer should be rejected]

In both, the parts joined by and/or are not syntactically alike — either in category or in function.

② Acceptable Coordination of Different Categories
Even when the categories are different, coordination is allowed if the function is the same. Look at these examples:

ⓐ He won't reveal [the nature of the threat or where it came from].
(NP + Clause → both are complements)
ⓑ I'll be back [next week or at the end of the month].
(NP + PP → both are time adjuncts)
ⓒ He acted [selfishly and with no thought for the consequences].
(AdvP + PP → both are manner adjuncts)
ⓓ They rejected the [United States and British] objections.
(Nominal + Adj → both are modifiers)

Functional Test

To check if coordination is acceptable, test whether each part can appear alone in the same position with the same function.

- He won't reveal the nature of the threat.
- He won't reveal where it came from.

Both are complements — coordination is allowed.

- I'll be back next week.
- I'll be back at the end of the month.

Both are time adjuncts — coordination is allowed.

③ Unacceptable Coordination Despite Matching Categories
In these examples, the categories match, but the functions do not, making coordination ungrammatical

* We're leaving [Rome and next week]. (NP + NP)
* I ran [to the park and for health reasons]. (PP + PP)

Why ungrammatical?

- We're leaving <u>Rome.</u> → object
- We're leaving <u>next week.</u> → time adjunct
- I ran <u>to the park</u>. → goal complement
- I ran <u>for health reasons</u>. → reason adjunct

Different functions — coordination not allowed.

- General Rule

A coordination of X and Y is allowed in a sentence only if both X and Y can appear individually in the same position with the same function.

Examples Satisfying the Rule

ⓐ We invited [Kim and Pat].
We invited Kim.
We invited Pat.
All are direct objects — coordination is valid.

ⓑ She is [very young and a quick learner].
She is very young.
She is a quick learner.
All are predicative complements — coordination is valid.

Coordination

- Relative Clause Coordination Must Be "Across the Board"

ⓐ They attended the dinner but they are not members. (main clause coordination)
ⓑ The people [who attended the dinner and who are not members] owe $20.
ⓒ * The people [who attended the dinner and they are not members] owe $20.

In ⓑ, both clauses are relative clauses → OK
In ⓒ, only the first clause is a relative clause, but the second is a full sentence → Not allowed

- Exception: Head + Dependent Constructions

These are not subject to the same coordination rules.

ⓐ They attended the dinner although they are not members.
ⓑ * The people [who attended the dinner although who are not members] owe $20.
ⓒ The people [who attended the dinner although they are not members] owe $20.

In ⓒ, although is not a coordinator — it introduces a dependent clause, so relativizing just the first part is fine.

Multiword Verbs

Multiword verbs are combinations of a lexical verb and one or more particles. A particle is a word that looks like an adverb or preposition but behaves differently in these combinations.

There are three main types:

① Phrasal verbs (verb + adverb particle)
  → drink up, find out
② Prepositional verbs (verb + preposition)
  → cope with, believe in
③ Phrasal-prepositional verbs (verb + adverb + preposition)
  → put up with, look forward to

1. Phrasal Verbs

Phrasal verbs are combinations of a verb and an adverb particle. Their meaning is often idiomatic, meaning it cannot be predicted from the meanings of the verb and the particle alone.

There are two main types of phrasal verbs:
- Intransitive (no object)
- Transitive (with an object)

① Intransitive Phrasal Verbs
These phrasal verbs do not take a direct object.

The plane has just touched down.
He is playing around.
I hope you'll get by.
She turned up unexpectedly.
The tank blew up.
The girls fell out. (= had a quarrel)

In many cases, the meaning of the whole verb phrase cannot be guessed by looking at the verb and particle separately.

Multiword Verbs

② Transitive Phrasal Verbs
These phrasal verbs take a direct object and can be:
Separable, Inseparable, Permanently separated

ⓐ Separable Transitive Phrasal Verbs
The verb and particle can be separated by the object.

They turned on the light.
They turned the light on.
She brought up two children.

- Particle Movement Rule
When the object is a pronoun, the particle must follow the object
They turned it on.
* They turned on it.

ⓑ Inseparable Transitive Phrasal Verbs
The verb and particle cannot be separated.

He ran across an old photo.
* He ran an old photo across.
She looks after her grandmother.
* She looks her grandmother after.

These verbs often have idiomatic meanings that cannot be understood literally.
come by (= acquire)
get over (= recover from)
look after (= take care of)
look into (= investigate)
stand by (= support)
run into (= encounter)

© Permanently Separated Transitive Phrasal Verbs
The object must always go between the verb and the particle. You cannot move the particle to another position.

The coach's attitude is getting the team down.
The judge let the thief off with a warning.

ask [someone] out (= invite)
do [something] over (= redo)
get [someone] down (= depress)
let [someone] off (= excuse/reduce punishment)
see [something] through (= complete)
string [someone] along (= deceive or mislead)
narrow [something] down (= reduce)

Multiword Verbs

2. Prepositional Verbs

Prepositional verbs are combinations of a lexical verb followed by a preposition. The verb and the preposition work together to form a single unit of meaning or grammatical structure.

Look at these pictures.
I don't care for Jane's parties.
We must go into the problem.
Can you cope with the work?
I approve of their action.
His eyes lighted upon the jewel.

・ Key Features
① Transitive Use
Prepositional verbs are usually transitive, meaning they take an object after the preposition.

② Preposition Cannot Be Moved
Unlike separable phrasal verbs, the preposition must always stay with the verb and cannot be separated from the object.

He applied for the job.
* He applied the job for.

③ Meaning is Often Transparent
In contrast to many phrasal verbs (which are idiomatic), the meaning of a prepositional verb is usually clear from the verb and the preposition.

3. Phrasal Prepositional Verbs

Phrasal Prepositional Verbs are multi-word verbs that consist of:
- a lexical verb
- an adverb particle
- a preposition

These three elements function together as a single verbal unit.

We are all looking forward to your party on Saturday.
He had to put up with a lot of teasing at school.
Why don't you look in on Mrs. Johnson on your way back?
He thinks he can get away with everything.

① Key Features
- Three-Part Structure

These verbs always include: → Verb + Adverb + Preposition

- Cannot Be Split

The three elements must stay together as a unit. The object comes after the preposition.

I have to put up with his attitude.
* I have to put his attitude up with.

- Idiomatic Meaning

The overall meaning of the phrase is often idiomatic, and cannot be guessed by analyzing each part separately.

put up with = tolerate
look forward to = eagerly anticipate
do away with = abolish
face up to = confront
look down on = despise

Multiword Verbs

② Passivization
Phrasal prepositional verbs can be passivized, but the results sometimes sound formal or awkward. However, some are common and natural in passive constructions:

I can't put up with his rudeness.
→ His rudeness can't be put up with.

They looked down on the new neighbors.
→ The new neighbors were looked down on by everyone.

We must face up to these problems.
→ These problems must be faced up to.

Society has done away with the death penalty.
→ The death penalty has been done away with.

③ Adverb Insertion
You can insert adverbs between the particles if needed, but the full verb structure must remain intact.

I haven't kept up fully with the class material.
* I haven't kept fully up with the class material.

4. The Distinction Between Prepositional Verbs and Phrasal Verbs

Prepositional verbs and phrasal verbs may look similar on the surface—both involve a lexical verb followed by a particle—but they differ in both syntax (sentence structure) and phonology (pronunciation and stress). Let's explore the key differences step by step.

Examples for Comparison

Type	Verb	Meaning	Example Sentence
Prepositional Verb	call on	to visit	She called on her friends.
Phrasal Verb	call up	to summon	She called up her friends.

Differences
① Position of Object and Particle
　・For prepositional verbs, the preposition must stay before the object.
She called on her friends.
* She called her friends on.

　・For phrasal verbs, the particle can move after the object.
She called up her friends.
She called her friends up.

② Personal Pronoun Placement
　・In prepositional verbs, the object pronoun must follow the preposition.
She called on them.
* She called them on.

　・In phrasal verbs, the object pronoun must come between the verb and the particle.
She called them up.
* She called up them.

③ Adverb Insertion
　・In prepositional verbs, adverbs (e.g. angrily, often) can be inserted between the verb and the preposition.
She called angrily on her friends.

　・In phrasal verbs, adverbs cannot normally be inserted between the verb and the particle.
* She called angrily up her friends.

Multiword Verbs

④ Relative and WH-Clauses
• With prepositional verbs, the preposition can move before a relative pronoun or WH-word.
The friends on whom she called.
On which friends did she call?

• With phrasal verbs, the particle cannot be moved before WH-elements.
* The friends up whom she called.
* Up which friends did she call?

⑤ Stress and Intonation
• In phrasal verbs, the particle is stressed, and when it's at the end of the sentence, it usually bears the nuclear tone (main pitch focus).
Which friends did she CALL on? (stress on "CALL")
• In prepositional verbs, the preposition is not stressed. The nuclear tone falls on the main verb, and the preposition has a reduced or "tail" tone.
Which friends did she call UP? (stress on "UP")

5. Type II Prepositional Verbs (Ditransitive): Passivization

Type II prepositional verbs are ditransitive verbs that take two noun phrases (NPs) as complements—typically with the second NP introduced by a preposition. These verbs allow passivization, though in a slightly different way than standard transitive verbs.

① Structure of Type II Prepositional Verbs
These verbs take the form:
- Verb + Direct Object + Preposition + Prepositional Object

② Passivization
In passives, it is typically the direct object (the first NP) that becomes the subject of the passive clause:
Active: The gang robbed her of her necklace.
Passive: She was robbed of her necklace (by the gang).

③ Examples of Type II Prepositional Verbs
Here are more examples with their passive counterparts:

They plied the young man with food.
→ The young man was plied with food.

Please confine your remarks to the topic.
→ Your remarks should be confined to the topic.

Jenny thanked us for the present.
→ We were thanked for the present.

They provided the child with a good education.
→ The child was provided with a good education.

May I remind you of our agreement?
→ May you be reminded of our agreement?

Multiword Verbs

④ Minor Subtypes
There are two minor subtypes where passivization works a bit differently.

ⓐ Subtype 1: Direct Object is Part of an Idiom
Some verbs form fixed expressions where the direct object is idiomatic, like

make a mess of
take care of
pay attention to
take advantage of

These expressions can sometimes be passivized in two ways—with the idiomatic NP or with the prepositional object as subject. However, the second version is less preferred.

Active: They made a terrible mess of the house.
Passive (preferred): A terrible mess was made of the house.
Passive (less acceptable): The house was made a terrible mess of.

ⓑ Subtype 2: Only the Prepositional Object Becomes Subject
Some idioms allow only the prepositional object to become the subject in the passive. These include:

catch sight of
lose touch with
give rise to
keep pace with
give way to
cross swords with
keep tabs on

Active: Suddenly, they caught sight of the lifeboat.
Passive: The lifeboat was caught sight of suddenly.

While grammatically correct, these passive sentences can sound awkward or clumsy, and are more often found in formal or literary writing.

Adjectives

1. Ordering of Adjectives in Premodification

When two or more adjectives are used to describe a noun (in attributive position—before the noun), their order follows a certain semantic hierarchy. This means adjectives are arranged in a specific order depending on what kind of meaning they express.

In English noun phrases, adjectives come after determiners (like a, the, my, some) but before the head noun.

• The Four Adjective Zones
We divide the position of adjectives in a noun phrase into four zones, moving closer and closer to the noun

① Precentral Zone
Meaning: Emphasizing or intensifying quality
Examples: certain, definite, sheer, complete, utter, mere

certain people, sheer nonsense, utter silence

② Central Zone
Meaning: General descriptive qualities (opinion, size, age, shape, etc.)
Examples: beautiful, funny, stupid, silent, hungry, huge, old

a funny story, a huge mistake

③ Postcentral Zone
Meaning: Participles or physical properties like color
Examples: broken, sleeping, retired, red, silver, striped

a sleeping baby, a red apple, striped pants

④ Prehead Zone
Meaning: Denominal adjectives—often used for classification, origin, material, or field
Examples: Austrian, Midwestern, scientific, political, economic, wood, metal

a political crisis, an Austrian dessert, a metal fence

• Putting It All Together: Expected Order
The general adjective order (based on the zones) is:
① (Precentral) → ② (Central) → ③ (Postcentral) → ④ (Prehead) → Noun

Example Combinations:
certain (①) + important (②) → certain important people
funny (②) + red (③) → a funny red hat
enormous (②) + tidal (④) → an enormous tidal wave
certain (①) + rich (②) + American (④) → certain rich American producers

Adjectives

2. Adjectives and Participles

The distinction between adjectives and participles is sometimes unclear because both -ing and -ed forms can act like either verbs or adjectives, depending on the context.

① When Participles Act as Verbs
A participle is clearly verbal when:
- The -ing form is used with a direct object.
- The -ed form is followed by a by-phrase with a personal agent.

Examples: Verbal Use
- -ing participle + object

Her views were alarming her audience.
You are frightening the children.
They are insulting us.

Here, the participles (alarming, frightening, insulting) form part of the verb phrase, not adjectives.

- -ed participle + personal agent (by-phrase)

The man was offended by the policeman.
He is appreciated by his students.
She was misunderstood by her parents.

In these cases, the -ed participles also act verbally, as they are part of a passive construction.

② When Participles Act as Adjectives
A participle is clearly adjectival when:
- It is preceded by the intensifier very.
- It is used without a verbal object or agent phrase.

Examples: Adjective Use with very

Her views were very alarming.
You are very frightening.
The man was very offended.

Here, the participles (alarming, frightening, offended) are clearly being used as adjectives, modifying the subject.

③ What Happens When very and a Verbal Context Co-occur?

ⓐ Unacceptable with -ing + object
If very is used with a verbal -ing participle that already has a direct object, the sentence becomes ungrammatical:

* His views were very alarming his audience.

This is because very suggests adjectival use, while "alarming his audience" is clearly verbal—causing a conflict.

ⓑ Borderline with -ed + personal agent
With -ed participles, using very and a personal by-phrase is sometimes accepted, though it may sound awkward

? The man was very offended by the policeman.

This kind of usage is becoming more acceptable in informal contexts.

ⓒ Acceptable with -ed + non-personal agent (cause)
Using very with a non-human cause in a by-phrase is generally acceptable

I'm very disturbed by your attitude.
We were very pleased by his behavior.

In these examples, the cause (e.g., your attitude, his behavior) helps the participle function more adjectivally, making very compatible.

Adjectives

3. Semantic Subclassification of Adjectives

Adjectives can be classified based on their meaning and behavior into two major dimensions: stative vs. dynamic, and gradable vs. nongradable. These categories help explain how adjectives behave in different syntactic environments.

① Stative vs. Dynamic Adjectives

ⓐ Stative Adjectives
Stative adjectives describe permanent or unchanging qualities or states. They do not typically occur:
- In the progressive aspect (be + being)
- In the imperative form (commands)

Examples of stative adjectives: tall, old, intelligent

* He's being tall.
* Be tall.

These are ungrammatical because tall is a stative adjective.

ⓑ Dynamic Adjectives
Dynamic adjectives describe temporary or changing conditions. Many of these adjectives involve subjective evaluation or emotional states. They can:
- Occur in the progressive aspect
- Be used in imperative sentences (more naturally than stative adjectives)

Examples

I didn't realize he was being funny.
Be brave. / Stop being greedy!

Common dynamic adjectives include: brave, calm, cheerful, conceited, cruel, foolish, friendly, funny, good, greedy, helpful, jealous, naughty, noisy, tidy

② Gradable vs. Nongradable Adjectives

ⓐ Gradable Adjectives
Gradable adjectives describe qualities that can vary in degree. They allow:
- Comparison: tall → taller → tallest
- Intensifiers: very tall, so beautiful, extremely useful

Examples

She is more beautiful than her sister.
This task is extremely difficult.

Gradability also applies to adverbs

He ran very quickly.
She answered more politely than before.

Most stative adjectives and all dynamic adjectives are gradable.

ⓑ Nongradable Adjectives
Nongradable adjectives describe absolute or categorical properties that do not vary by degree. They do not allow comparison or intensification.

Examples of nongradable adjectives

atomic (as in atomic scientist)
hydrochloric (as in hydrochloric acid)
British, Korean, Victorian

These are usually:
- Denominal adjectives (derived from nouns)
- Adjectives of origin or type

* very atomic
* more British
Such uses are generally ungrammatical.

Summary

Category	Definition	Examples	Can Use "Very"?	Can Compare?	Can Use Progressive?
Stative	Describes stable, permanent states	tall, old, British	○(if gradable)	○(if gradable)	×
Dynamic	Describes temporary, subjective, or emotional conditions	funny, greedy, brave	○	○	○
Gradable	Can vary in intensity or degree	tall, useful, beautiful	○	○	Depends (if dynamic)
Nongradable	Absolute qualities or categories	atomic, hydrochloric, British	×	×	×

Adjectives

4. The Unmarked Term in Measure Expressions

In English, certain adjectives and adverbs are used as default (unmarked) terms in measure expressions, especially when we ask about or describe measurements. These forms are used even when the intended meaning is not at the extreme end of the scale.

① The Case of Old
The adjective old is used in expressions of age, no matter whether the person is actually old or young

Mr. Jespersen is 75 years old.
His granddaughter is two years old.

In these examples, old functions simply to describe someone's age. Even though two years is very young, old is used because it is the unmarked term on the age scale. This means it's the default adjective used, even for young people.

She is two years old. = Her age is two years.

② Unmarked vs. Marked Terms
In pairs of adjectives with opposite meanings, one is typically unmarked (neutral, used in general questions or descriptions), while the other is marked (used to emphasize one end of the scale).

• Common Adjective Pairs

Unmarked	Marked
old	young
deep	shallow
high	low
long	short
tall	short
thick	thin
wide	narrow

Unmarked examples

How old is she? (= What is her age?)
How deep is the lake? (= What is the depth?)

These questions do not assume that someone is old or that something is deep—they are neutral.

- More Unmarked Adjectives and Adverbs

Other adjectives and adverbs also function as unmarked terms in questions

- Adjective Examples

Unmarked	Marked
big	small
bright	dim
fat	thin
heavy	light
large	little
strong	weak

How heavy is your computer?
How accurate is that clock?
How much does it cost?
How far did you drive today?

These are neutral questions, asking for specific values without assuming extremes.

③ Marked Terms in Questions and Exclamations
When we use a marked term in a question (e.g., young), we presuppose something about the situation.

- Compare

How old is John?
→ Neutral: Just asking for his age.
How young is John?
→ Presupposes that John is young, and asks how young he is.

- In exclamations, neither form is neutral

How young he is! → Emphasizes extreme youth.
How old he is! → Emphasizes extreme age.

Adjectives

5. Attributive-Only Adjectives

Some adjectives in English can only appear before nouns—that is, in attributive position—and not after linking verbs like be. These are called attributive-only adjectives.

a former president
* The president is former.

Compare these two
He saw one of his former wives.
→ former appears before the noun → OK.
He saw one of his wives who is former.
→ former appears after the noun → Not acceptable.

Some other attributive-only adjectives include:
drunken, erstwhile, eventual, future, mere, principal, utter

She thought that he was an utter fool.
* He was utter.

- Types of Attributive-Only Adjectives

① Adjectives of Degree
These describe the extent or intensity of the head noun, often in absolute terms.

an utter disaster
a complete failure
sheer nonsense
a total moron

These adjectives do not describe a quality of the noun directly but rather emphasize the degree of it.

② Quantifying Adjectives
These describe amount, quantity, or frequency.

the only option
the entire crew
an occasional visitor
the usual suspects

Again, these do not describe a property of the noun, but provide information about number or frequency.

③ Adjectives of Time and Location
These adjectives relate the noun to a time frame or place.

a future meeting
his former job
a previous version
her left arm
the northeastern provinces

In many cases, these cannot appear in predicative position (* Her arm is left).

④ Associative Adjectives
These do not describe an inherent property of the noun, but describe what the noun is associated with.

a nuclear physicist (not a "nuclear" person!)
a criminal lawyer (not a lawyer who is criminal)
a public official
a mathematical journal
a moral dilemma

These adjectives simply tell what field or category the noun belongs to.

⑤ Adjective Compounds
These are adjective phrases made of two words. Many are attributive-only, and their parts can be from different word classes (e.g., noun + participle).

a grayish-blue car (adjective + adjective)
a big-name director (adjective + noun)
a clean-shaven man (adjective + past participle compound)
a glass-bottom boat (noun + noun)
a world-renowned scientist (noun + participle)

Some of these cannot be used after a linking verb
His car is grayish-blue.
* The director is big-name.
* The boat is glass-bottom.

The scientist is world renowned. (Notice it is written as two words in this position.)

• Why Are These Adjectives Attributive-Only?
Sometimes, these adjectives describe a temporary role, an association, or a contextual degree, rather than a core property of the noun. Because of that, they can't stand alone as predicates.

His new friend is kind.
His friend is new. → unacceptable (if "new" means recently acquired, not inherently "new" in age or status)

Adverbials

In English grammar, adverbials are elements in a sentence that give extra information about time, manner, place, frequency, degree, reason, or viewpoint.

1. Subjuncts

Subjuncts are a type of adverbial that play a subordinate or parenthetical role in a sentence, unlike adjuncts, which are more central. Subjuncts either
- Widely relate to the whole sentence (→ wide orientation) but still show a close link with an element like the subject.
- Narrowly relate to part of the predication (→ narrow orientation).

① Wide Orientation Subjuncts
These refer to the sentence as a whole and are usually placed initially (I-position).

ⓐ Viewpoint Subjuncts
They express the speaker's viewpoint or the aspect/respect from which the sentence should be interpreted.
- Typically nongradable adverbs or prepositional phrases.
- Often occur at the beginning of the sentence.

Architecturally, the plans are impressive.
From a personal viewpoint, he'll do well.
Weatherwise, things look bad.

Compare
- Scientifically, the expedition was planned. [Subjunct]
(e.g., "From a scientific point of view...")
- The expedition was planned scientifically. [Adjunct - describes manner]
(e.g., "It was planned using scientific methods.")

ⓑ Courtesy Subjuncts
Used for politeness, often occur in medial position (M-position).
- Words like please, kindly, cordially, politely.
- Often formulaic or conventional expressions.

You are cordially invited.
He kindly offered his seat. (= He was kind to offer it.)

Compare
She offered her seat kindly. (Adjunct = in a kind way)

② Narrow Orientation Subjuncts
These relate specifically to a part of the predication, typically the subject.

ⓐ Item Subjuncts
They show the subject's attitude or manner in performing the action. Unlike manner adjuncts, they are often placed initially (I) or medially (M) and refer to the subject's disposition, not how the action was carried out.

- Consistently, she opposed the lawyers.
→ She was consistent in her opposition.

- Intentionally, they told him nothing.
→ They were intentional about not telling him.

- With great pride, he accepted the award.
→ He was very proud to accept the award.

- Deliberately, he misled us.
→ He was being deliberate when he misled us.

- With great unease, they elected him.
→ They were uneasy about the decision when they elected him.

Adverbials

2. Disjuncts

Disjuncts are adverbials that express the speaker's comment on the sentence. Unlike adjuncts (which are part of the action) or subjuncts (which modify parts of the clause), disjuncts are logically separate from the sentence. They often stand above or outside the main clause in meaning and reflect the speaker's stance on how or why the sentence is being said.

- Two Main Types of Disjuncts

① Style Disjuncts
These comment on the manner or source of what is being said.
They clarify under what authority, attitude, or perspective the speaker is making the statement.

Common Forms	Meaning / Function	Examples
Frankly, Honestly, Personally, Strictly, Technically	Show personal stance or framing	Frankly, I don't care. = "I tell you frankly..."
From my perspective, To be honest, If I may say so	Introduce the speaker's style or basis	From my personal observation, Mr. Forster neglects his children.

② Content Disjuncts
These comment on the truth, certainty, or evaluation of the content of the sentence.

ⓐ Disjuncts of Certainty
- These show the speaker's level of certainty or doubt about the truth of the statement.
- Can include adverbs like:

undoubtedly, probably, apparently, maybe, perhaps
- Or prepositional/clausal phrases like:

In essence, According to the report, If that's true, Since she was late...

The play was undoubtedly written by Francis Beaumont.
→ The speaker expresses strong certainty.

Since she had no time to fix the car, Rachel called a taxi.
→ The reason/cause is explained.

ⓑ Disjuncts of Evaluation
- These reflect a value judgment or personal stance about the whole proposition.

They may either:
- Comment on the subject's action or choice:

Wisely, Foolishly, Justly, Rightly, Stupidly, etc.
- Express a general attitude without commenting on the subject:

Naturally, Curiously, Surprisingly, Fortunately, Sadly, etc.

Wisely, Mrs. Jensen consulted her lawyer.
→ Mrs. Jensen's action is judged positively.

Naturally, my husband expected me home.
→ The situation itself is evaluated as expected — not the husband himself.

To my regret, she didn't apply.
→ A personal attitude is expressed via a prepositional phrase.

Sample Sentences Analysis

ⓐ The prisoner answered the questions foolishly.
→ [Adjunct] — This modifies how the prisoner answered (manner).
→ = He answered in a foolish manner.

ⓑ Foolishly, the prisoner answered the questions.
→ [Disjunct] — This comments on the entire act; it was unwise of him.
→ = It was foolish of him to answer them.

ⓒ Wisely, he answered the question foolishly.
→ [Disjunct / Adjunct] — The first adverb (wisely) is a disjunct: he made a smart choice to answer.
→ The second (foolishly) is an adjunct: he used a foolish manner in answering.
→ = He made a wise decision, but answered in a foolish tone/style.

Aspect

Aspect is a grammatical category that reflects how the action of a verb is viewed with respect to time. Unlike tense, which locates an event in time (past or present), aspect describes the nature or structure of the event itself — whether it is ongoing, completed, habitual, etc.

In English, there are two primary aspects:
 • Progressive aspect: Indicates that an action is ongoing (e.g., She is running.)
 • Perfect aspect: Indicates that an action is completed with relevance to another time (e.g., She has run five miles.)

These two aspects can be combined with either present or past tense to produce four common forms:

Tense	Progressive	Perfect	Perfect Progressive
Present	is running	has run	has been running
Past	was running	had run	had been running

1. Four Basic Aspectual Classes

Verbs can be classified into four major aspectual (lexical aspect) classes, based on the nature of the action or state they describe.

① States
Describe situations that are static, ongoing, and do not involve deliberate action or inherent change.
 • No natural endpoint.
 • Usually describe conditions or mental/emotional states.
 • Subjects are not typically agents of action.

Roger had a rash.
Karen felt happy.
Nora liked the book.

② Activities
Describe dynamic actions that are ongoing and do not have a defined endpoint.
 • Can continue indefinitely.(not having any natural endpoints.)
 • Often involve deliberate or repeated action.

Karen talked to Martha.
Martin wandered around.
Mavis snored.

③ Accomplishments
Describe actions that are processes with a clear endpoint.
- Involve change over time.
- Have a built-in goal or completion point.

Dorothy built a house. (endpoint = house is finished)
Georgia wrote a sonnet.
Ron peeled the carrot.

④ Achievements
Describe actions or events that happen instantaneously and are centered on a single endpoint.
- Momentary or punctual.
- Often involve a sudden change of state.

Joel arrived at the meeting.
Fred's goldfish died.
Linda finished her dissertation.

2. Rules Concerning Aspectual Adverbial Phrases

Adverbial phrases headed by in and for are frequently used to mark the duration of an event or state. However, they behave differently depending on the aspectual class of the verb phrase they modify.

ⓐ Two Uses of "in + time" Phrases
Phrases like in four minutes can have two distinct meanings

- Aspectual (Duration): Refers to how long an event takes from beginning to end.

Roger Bannister will run a mile in four minutes.
→ It will take him four minutes to finish running a mile.

- Relational (Onset): Refers to the time before the event begins.

Roger Bannister will run a mile in four minutes.
→ He will begin running four minutes from now.

ⓑ Compatibility with Aspectual Classes
- "in + time" phrases are natural with

Accomplishments and Achievements (actions with natural endpoints).

Ron peeled the carrot in three minutes. [Accomplishment]
Linda finished her thesis in three months. [Achievement]

Aspect

- "for + time" phrases are natural with
States and Activities (actions with no defined endpoint).

Roger had a rash for three days. [State]
Karen talked to Martha for thirty minutes. [Activity]

③ Diagnostic Test: "for" vs. "in" to Identify Aspectual Class
Using "for X time" and "in X time" helps diagnose the aspectual class of a verb phrase:

Simon treated Roger's rash...
...for three weeks → Activity
...in three weeks → X

Simon healed Roger's rash...
...in three weeks → Accomplishment
...for three weeks → X

This test shows that treating is an activity, and healing is an accomplishment.

④ Motion Verbs: Goal = Accomplishment, No Goal = Activity

Brenda drove to San Francisco in an hour. [Accomplishment: definite goal]
Brenda drove toward San Francisco for an hour. [Activity: no definite goal]

Gordon rowed two miles in an hour. [Accomplishment: definite distance]
Gordon rowed for an hour. [Activity: no specific endpoint]

Motion verb phrases that reach a specific goal or cover a definite distance are treated as accomplishments or achievements. Otherwise, they are activities.

⑤ Object Specificity Determines Class
- Definite object → Accomplishment
- Indefinite/mass object → Activity

Accomplishment	Activity
Freddy ate a pancake in two minutes.	Freddy ate pancakes for two hours.
Linda drank a glass of beer in thirty seconds.	Linda drank beer for thirty minutes.
Frances read a story in thirty minutes.	Frances read stories for three hours.
Grant wrote a poem in three weeks.	Grant wrote poetry for three months.

If a verb phrase contains a definite direct object and is an accomplishment, then replacing it with an indefinite/mass noun object yields an activity.

3. In Adverbials: A Test for Telicity

① What is Telicity?
Telicity refers to whether an event or situation has a natural endpoint:
- Telic = has a built-in endpoint (e.g., build a house)
- Atelic = does not have a natural endpoint (e.g., walk in the park)

② The "In X Time" Test
The "in X minutes" adverbial test helps distinguish telic vs. atelic predicates
- Telic predicates (especially accomplishments and achievements) can combine with 'in X time.'
- Atelic predicates (states and activities) typically sound unnatural with 'in X time.'

ⓐ Telic: Accomplishments
With accomplishments, "in X time" measures event duration (from start to end)

He can eat a meat pie in 60 seconds.
They built the barn in two days.
Jones walked to town in 45 minutes.

ⓑ Telic: Achievements
Achievements do not have duration. "In X time" here refers to the delay before the event

He recognized her in a minute or so.
Jones noticed the marks in five minutes.
Jones lost his keys in three days.

Better phrasing for naturalness: use "within X time" for achievements.

ⓒ Atelic: States
"In X time" sounds anomalous or very awkward.

The couple were happy in two years.
The room was sunny in an hour.
Jones knew him well in five years.

Some can be interpreted as "It took X time before the state began" but remain odd.

ⓓ Atelic: Activities (Processes)
These do not have endpoints, so "in X time" is usually ungrammatical.

\# They walked in the park in half an hour.
\# People chatted in half an hour.
\# Jones pushed a trolley in 90 seconds.

Sentence (Jones knew him well in five years.) might be okay only if interpreted telically, e.g., pushing a trolley across a finish line.

- Future Tense Exception

With future tense, any predicate can co-occur with "in X time," because it is interpreted as "X time before the event starts".

State: They will be happy in a year.
Process: We will walk in the park in an hour.
Accomplishment: They'll build the barn in two weeks.
Achievement: He will recognize her in a minute.

These are all acceptable in future tense but do not help diagnose telicity.

Key Takeaways

Predicate Type	Can Take "in X Time"?	Interpretation
State	No	Sounds awkward or ungrammatical
Activity	No	Sounds awkward; no defined endpoint
Accomplishment	Yes	Measures duration of event
Achievement	Yes (with care)	Time before event occurs; event = instant

Always use simple past tense to test telicity accurately.

Aspectual Class Comparison Table

Aspectual Class	Definition	Telic (Has Endpoint?)	Duration	Progressive Form?	Typical Verbs / Phrases
State	Static conditions, emotions, possession, etc.	×	○	× (Rarely acceptable)	know, love, believe, own, need
Activity	Ongoing or repeated actions with no inherent goal	×	○	○	run, walk, talk, swim, read (stories), watch TV
Accomplishment	Actions involving a process with a clear goal or result	○	○	○	build a house, write a letter, eat a cake, read a book
Achievement	Instantaneous events with a sudden change of state	○	×	× (Generally not)	arrive, win, find, recognize, notice, reach

문제 및 정답

강의자료실과 다음카페어
문제 및 정답 업로드하였습니다
강의자료실 또는 다음카페에서 다운받아
문제를 풀어주시기 바랍니다.

허 은 성

단국대 영어영문학과 학사 졸업
경기대 교육대학원 영어교육전공 석사 졸업
California State Polytechnic University, Pomona 교환학생
영어 정교사 자격증
現 희소쌤플러스 전공영어 강사
前 경기도교육청 공무원
前 천재교육 교과서 전략팀
공무원 영어 강의
임용고시 전공영어 강의

허은성 전공영어
영어학 2

초 판 1쇄 인쇄 2025년 4월 8일
초 판 1쇄 발행 2025년 4월 11일

편 저 자 허 은 성
발 행 인 이 중 수
발 행 처 동 문 사

서울특별시 서대문구 홍제원 1길 12 (홍제동 137-8)
Tel.   02)736-3718(대), 736-3710, 3720
Fax.   02)736-3719
E-mail dong736@naver.com
홈페이지 www.dongmunsa.com
등록번호 1974.04.27. 제9-17호
ISBN   979-11-6328-677-6 (13370)
가 격   20,000원

저자와의 합의하에 인지는 생략합니다.